MARKETING GREATEST HITS VOLUME II

MARKETING GREATEST HITS VOLUME II

ANOTHER MASTERCLASS IN MODERN MARKETING IDEAS

KEVIN DUNCAN

BLOOMSBURY

First published in Great Britain 2012 by

Bloomsbury Publishing Plc
50 Bedford Square
London
WC1B 3DP

A CIP record for this book is available from the British Library.

ISBN: 9-781-4081-5721-3

This book is produced using paper that is made from wood grown in
managed, sustainable forests. It is natural, renewable and recyclable.
The logging and manufacturing processes conform to the
environmental regulations of the country of origin.

Design by Fiona Pike, Pike Design, Winchester
Typeset by Saxon Graphics Ltd, Derby DE21 4SZ
Printed in Great Britain by Clays Ltd, St Ives plc

Dedicated to Sarah, Rosanna and Shaunagh.

Where to go next

For free updates and material, visit greatesthitsblog.com.

For apps, training products and other ideas,
visit expertadviceonline.com.

Contact the author at kevinduncan@expertadvice.co.uk.

Also by the author:
Business Greatest Hits
Catch-11
Marketing Greatest Hits
Revolution
Run Your Own Business
Small Business Survival
So What?
Start
Tick Achieve
What You Need to Know About Starting a Business

CONTENTS

CHAPTER 1.
THE BIG ISSUES:
CHAOS AND
EMOTION IN A
CROWDED
WORLD

Too much of everything

HOT, FLAT, AND CROWDED, THOMAS FRIEDMAN
We might as well start big, and there's no bigger than the world itself. Hard on the heels of *The World Is Flat* (2005), three-time Pulitzer prize-winning author Thomas Friedman pulled another classic out of the hat in 2009. No wonder he has been variously described as a global star and a zeitgeist thermometer. It is subtitled *Why the world needs a green revolution and how we can renew our global future,* which pretty much describes what it's about.

Climate change and rapid population growth mean that it's no longer possible for businesses, or the rest of us, to keep doing things the same old way, he says. We need to change, and fast. He provides a bold strategy for clean fuel, energy efficiency and conservation that he calls '*Code Green*'. This is to counteract growing demand for energy and resources, the transfer of wealth to oil-rich countries, climate change, energy poverty, and accelerating biodiversity loss.

The title is based on the fact that the world is now in danger of being hot (due to global warming), flat (due to the rise of high-consuming middle classes all over the world) and crowded (adding about a billion people every 13 years). He analyses when the market and Mother Nature hit the wall, showing that the parallels between the two phenomena are eerie.

IBG (I'll be gone) and YBG (You'll be gone) are simple acronyms referring to those who are exploiting people and financial markets – they won't be around to suffer the consequences, so they don't really give a damn. Their approach is to privatise gains and socialise loss – those doing the exploiting benefit from any gains, and the taxpayer pays if there's a loss.

A World Wildlife Fund Living Planet Report in 2008 concluded that we are already operating 25 per cent above the planet's biological capacity to support life. As a result, Friedman names us the *Grasshopper Generation* – eating our way through a staggering amount of wealth and resources in a short period of time. To an extent this is a call to arms for a change in our approach to economics, consumption and lifestyle, but it also has significant implications for business.

The one-sentence summary
**Geographical boundaries have effectively
disappeared where business is concerned.**

In case you think he's exaggerating, he suggests you key the words 'world population' into Google and add the year of your birth. In 1950 there were 2.5 billion on the planet; today there are 6.8 billion, with 9 billion predicted by 2050. (Friedman wrote this in 2009, and by now this figure has reached 7 billion). So within 40 years the figure will rise by the world's entire 1950 population. These are serious figures. In the last 20 years the world market has more than doubled from three to over six billion. New entrants crave the spoils previously only enjoyed by the western world, and they are getting their hands on it fast.

From a business perspective, this certainly offers a volume opportunity in one direction, but it also means intense competitive pressure in the other. A huge reservoir of labour and intelligence has been released, which allows an American to leave the office in the evening and have a presentation written overnight in India sitting on his or her desk by the morning. Geographical boundaries have in many respects disappeared. Marketing initiatives can therefore take advantage of a much broader canvas than before – bigger markets and more consumers. The BRIC countries – Brazil, Russia, India and China – offer a case in point.

Unsurprisingly, this is an ultra-short and oversimplified summary of the whole. *Hot, Flat, and Crowded* is very long and detailed, and so is not for the faint-hearted. But it's worth the ride, because it sets in context pretty much every other issue we might want to look at.

If everything is all over the place, what can you do?

CHAOTICS, KOTLER & CASLIONE

After the financial meltdown of 2008, business guru Philip Kotler got together with John A. Caslione to develop the *Chaotics Management System*. Most business books these days have a subtitle, and this one is *The Business of Managing Marketing in the Age of Turbulence*. Their start point is that turbulence is not an aberration, but the new norm in business. That the recent economic downturn is simply part of a continually oscillating Age of Turbulence, where both risk and opportunity are felt quickly round the world, which is now inexorably linked by globalism and technology. This is a brutally competitive world market that chews up the unprepared but rewards the prepared, so those companies robust enough to anticipate quickly and respond effectively will do best.

To cope with all this, they designed the *Chaotics Management System* to help companies minimise vulnerability and exploit opportunities fast. Panic tactics such as staff cuts, price reductions and slashed investment don't work, but early-warning systems do. Factors that cause chaos are technological advances, the information revolution, disruptive technologies, the rise of the rest, hypercompetition, sovereign wealth funds, the environment and customer empowerment. Companies need to be responsive, robust and resilient. The most common mistakes made are:

1. *Stretching to attract new customers before you've secured the core*

2. *Cutting marketing*

3. *Neglecting the 900lb gorilla (everyone knows you're in trouble, so admit it)*

The one-sentence summary

Turbulence is the new normal – get used to it and develop early-warning systems.

The *Chaotics* system has three main components:

1. Detect sources of turbulence through early-warning systems

The first signs of upheaval, disruptive innovations and shocks can be seen in advance with the right preparation.

2. Respond to chaos by constructing key scenarios

Draw up detailed worst-case, best-case and most-expected-case scenarios, with strategies for dealing effectively with each one.

3. Select strategy based on scenario prioritisation and risk attitude

Acting fast, based on pre-agreed approaches, builds resilience into the business.

Chaos inflection points can render a strategy obsolete overnight. That's a moment when turbulence suddenly changes everything. The best response is 'skill, will, till':

Skill: increase spending on new customers
Will: have a culture to go against the trend
Till: have some resources to invest

The book includes plenty of process charts and diagrams that you can map out and enact. Anyone can ask the critical questions:

- **What have been our past blind spots?**

- **Is there an analogy from another industry?**

- **What signals are we rationalising away?**

- **Who is skilled at picking up weak signals and acting on them?**

- **What are our mavericks and outliers trying to tell us?**

- **What future surprises could really hurt or help us?**

The key lies in providing totally honest answers to the questions, and working out in advance what can be done if the worst happens – a form of disaster planning. Business leaders need to see change first hand, eliminate the filers (people who file things away) that stop them finding out fast, accept the inevitability of strategy decay, and drop their reliance on a two-playbook strategy – one for up markets and the other for down.

There are some interesting thoughts here. We have all seen businesses that only plan for the up-a-bit, down-a-bit year. In truth, a year of constant turbulence may well be more realistic. Those at the top of companies would do well to be aware of staff who 'file things away'. The only way to find out about potential problems is to be very well informed. This is perhaps easier said than done.

As with most Kotler, *Chaotics* is reasonably serious stuff, so there is precious little levity to sugar the pill. Laid out in classic American style, there are perfectly manageable chunks to get to grips with, but you really have to get stuck into the charts if you intend to implement the methodology.

It's a big issue – no, it's a small issue

THE LITTLE BIG THINGS, TOM PETERS

Ever since his world dominating *In Search of Excellence* (1982), Tom Peters has been a colossus of the business world. He is never short of an opinion, and the flyleaf of his latest book, *The Little Big Things* (2010), modestly describes *In Search of Excellence* as the business book that changed the world. In truth, after all this time most of his work is a variation of his general philosophy and, as such, this is not a book with a cohesive theme in the traditional sense – it contains 163 ways to pursue excellence, originally published as a series of blogs. The author has a passion for little stories that illustrate the larger point, and loves telling them.

His overall theme is that it's the soft things that matter, and they are very hard to do. This is a close cousin of the Ludwig Mies van der Rohe aphorism that *'God is in the details'*, so beloved of designers the world over. Peters sees this as the binding theme throughout all his work – hundreds of small acts of humanity add up to big improvements in operational effectiveness for any company. He brings this thinking right up to date by comparing it to the new discipline of Behavioural Economics (see next chapter). Outcomes for businesses often tally with the fine line between rationality and irrationality, and that often means a dramatic overreaction to some tiny thing, or an under reaction to a big thing. Either way, marketers need to concentrate on this precariously balanced area if they want to avoid nasty repercussions for their brands.

It isn't possible to specify all 163 themes here, but we can draw out some recurring arguments. One characteristic that can help us when dealing with random events (Nassim Nicholas Taleb's *Black Swans*) is resilience, usually demonstrated by people with inner calm, high self-knowledge and a sense of humour. These people are vital to the success of any service business. Despite what many businesspeople will tell you, big change really *can* be achieved in a short space of time. Actually, it will take precisely as long as you think it will (those in highly bureaucratic companies may beg to differ with this). On the other hand, big plans don't work – it is small steps that get things done. He has a particular go at *planners,* who he says announce good intentions but don't motivate anyone to carry them out. If you have the word planner in your title, you may take offence at this, but in fact he is defining a character type rather than a job specification. On the other hand, *searchers* find things that work and build on them, with more effective results. In this respect, he believes that serious play beats serious planning, because all practical ideas evolve from prototypes.

The one-sentence summary

It's the soft things that matter, and they are very hard to do.

Peters references Seth Godin, who says that if you can't describe your position in eight words or less, you don't have a position. Peters call this an RPOV *(Remarkable Point of View)*. All businesses, and people, should have one. The thoughts keep coming, including:

1. **Kindness is free, so deploy it more often**

2. **To Don't lists are often more important than To Do lists**
   Over half of what we do is unnecessary.

3. **Leaders should practice Servant Leadership**
   What did I specifically do today to be of service to my people?

4. **Staff are a more important audience than the customer**
   If they are not happy and motivated, then the customer won't be either, so it starts on the inside.

5. **Apology is one of the most powerful tools at any company's disposal**

6. **Don't learn from your failures**
   Look for things that went right and build on them.

From a stylistic viewpoint, the book is riddled with exclamation marks (over 60 on the inside cover and contents pages alone), which could prove irritating to those who favour a more sedate, less dramatic, read. There is also a fair amount of repetition which suggests a more rigorous edit could have been embarked upon, but this may be because the publisher who persuaded him to convert his blogs into a book decided to leave them pretty much in their original online form.

When facts are not facts

THE SPIRIT LEVEL DELUSION, CHRISTOPHER SNOWDON
It's always fun when someone writes a book saying that another, or several of them, are a load of rubbish. It happened in 2007 when Phil Rozenzweig wrote *The Halo Effect*, in which he comprehensively denounced the classics (*In Search of Excellence, Good to Great* and *Built to Last*) as little more than storytelling. A similar thing happened in 2010, when Christoper Snowdon unleashed *The Spirit Level Delusion.* A number of high-selling books, including *The Spirit Level (2009), Affluenza (2007)* and *The Selfish Capitalist (2008),* had made extraordinary claims in favour of big government, calling for a radical shift in power from the individual to the state. Snowdon was not happy about it.

In his opinion, the claims they make are based on the supposedly devastating effects of wealth, economic growth and inequality, but he goes on to show that the theory not only lacks empirical support but also fails the basic test of believability. The original *The Spirit Level* authors, Wilkinson & Pickett, believe that more equal societies do better, and try to prove the point by showing higher rates of suicide, crime, mental illness and infant mortality (and lower rates of happiness) in unequal ones. *The Spirit Level Delusion* works methodically through all these claims, and pretty much discredits every one of them.

Mixed methodologies and pick 'n' mix data are major culprits – Wilkinson & Pickett effectively only choose the bits that suit them. All anti-consumerist tracts end up recommending higher taxes, more government and fresh prohibition, regardless of where they start, says Snowdon. That could be mental health (*Affluenza* – Oliver James); shopping (*All Consuming* – Neal Lawson); health (*Status Syndrome* – Michael Marmot); or quality of life (*Happiness* – Richard Layard). It makes for interesting reading to work through 40 or 50 graphs that have been used to support a case, only to find that they have used selective data, drawn inappropriate conclusions, or claimed causality where there is none.

The one-sentence summary
We live in a complex world of infinite subtleties and variation – don't try to attribute causality when there is none.

The book is keen to stress that, unlike many business books, it contains no big idea. Instead, it is a careful look at the data presented by others, to see if it says what they claim. This is a salutary lesson in remembering that those of us who are not natural mathematicians should not be bamboozled by those who put up seemingly authoritative graphs and attribute certain findings to them – the data may be saying nothing of the sort. Trends and correlations are a tricky area here. Changing the scale of a graph, excluding one outlier, including another outlier – all can skew the picture in one move.

The book tries very hard to be neutral, and in the main, succeeds. Nevertheless it is a response with a stance, so you have to aim off for that. It concludes only that we live in a complex world of infinite subtleties and variation, and that the future lies in improving material conditions for all rather than forcibly protecting individuals from their own emotions. It openly admits that some level of status anxiety exists, but suggests that it is overstated. Status anxiety is one of the biggest points made by those believing that inequality causes greater mental stress.

In an amusing anecdote from Dr John Lynch, he suggests that only an advocate of the psychosocial theory would suggest that seeing the bigger seats when leaving an aircraft created the difference between flying economy or first class, rather than the more obvious tangible benefits. Snowdon's dismantling of the evidence makes for great reading. To illustrate the daftness of some of the causations supposedly drawn, he produces a thoroughly plausible graph to show the relationship between educational achievement and proximity to the North Pole. It is statistically accurate, but although there is a mathematical correlation, there is of course no causality. After one particularly robust deconstruction of data, he concludes that *'this mind-boggling combination of rhetorical tricks and non sequiturs suggests an unfulfilled career as a defence lawyer'.* It is well written, but with a very serious point.

Are feelings more important than facts?

EMOTIONOMICS, DAN HILL

Dan Hill is a recognised authority on the role of emotions in consumer and employee behaviour, and an expert on analysing facial coding as an aid to measuring people's decision-making processes, particularly when testing customer insights. In 2008 he produced *Emotionomics,* which purported to explain the art of reading emotions for business advantage. He was in good company, and drew praise from Seth Godin, Martin Lindstrom, Paco Underhill and Philip Kotler among others (all featured elsewhere in this book in their own right).

His stance is that for too long emotions have been ignored in favour of rationality and efficiency, but breakthroughs in brain science have revealed that people are primarily emotional decision-makers. Companies need to catch up with this new thinking. Facial coding is the single best viable means of measuring and managing the emotional response of customers and employees. Science, psychology and economics now combine to move us forward: discovery of the brain's hot button (1986), articulation of emotional intelligence (1995), the positive psychology movement (1998), and Behavioural Economics (2002).

Behavioural Economics (see next chapter) is hard to summarise succinctly, but he offers a way, based on two main areas: categorisation and loss aversion. Categorisation tricks we engage in for emotional reasons are:

1. Framing

Making a choice more attractive by deliberately comparing it with inferior options.

2. **Mental accounting**
   Placing artificial limits on the amounts we are willing to spend in certain categories.

3. **Prospect theory**
   Judging pleasure based on a change in condition, rather than on how happy we are.

4. **Anchoring**
   Evaluating new information strictly in terms of what our baseline of knowledge happens to be.

5. **Recency**
   Giving undue weight to recent experiences.

The second element is loss aversion. Negative emotions are linked to survival and so are much stronger, which is why people feel more pain from loss than pleasure from profit. Aspects of loss aversion include:

1. **Familiarity**
   Having a bias towards the status quo.

2. **New-risk premium**
   Inflating the cost of accepting new risks while casually discounting familiar risks.

3. **Fear of regret**
   Suffering from having to admit a mistake.

4. **Decision paralysis**
   Failing to make a decision when faced with lots of choices for fear of making the wrong one.

This is a lot to take in. From a marketing perspective, companies have made some progress in using framing (good, better, best is an example) and recency (seasonal advertising), but have been less good at understanding mental accounting and anchoring. Probably their most clear-cut shortcoming is the way in which confusing line extensions and relentless addition of features has exacerbated decision paralysis.

The one-sentence summary
Emotion lies at the heart of consumer behaviour, so it is important to understand exactly how people decide what to buy.

The *Facial Action Coding System* categorises the activity of 43 facial muscles. These betray four core motivations: defend, acquire, bond and learn, which dovetail with core emotions: anger, happiness, sadness, fear, disgust and surprise. The lists keep coming; reasons for emotional resistance include: insecurity, powerlessness, dread, betrayal, exhaustion, defeat and injustice. It's a bit of a minefield and it probably takes an expert to work it all out.

What is evident is that brand equity is emotional and is hard to measure using rational attributes. Neurons that fire together wire together, he says – branding occurs only in the mind. Neurogenesis is the creation of new neurons throughout life, a process that confirms that we are not set in our ways. This means we can adopt and learn new ways of behaviour, and come to regard them as normal or habitual. Mirror neurons make us mimic and empathise, which is why you start to yawn when you see someone yawn, even if it's on the train and you don't know them.

If this is all somewhat baffling, it can probably be summarised most simply by reference to Wundt's curve. William Wundt was a psychologist who discovered that people respond differently to certain combinations of information. This means that maximum appeal occurs when a simple idea is presented in a novel way, or a complex idea is introduced in a familiar manner.

Motivation is not all about the money

DRIVE, DANIEL PINK

Daniel Pink has achieved international fame as a commentator on how the world works. In 2006 his book *A Whole New Mind* explained how creative right-brain thinkers would rule the future. In 2009 *Drive* took this to a new level, revealing the surprising truth about what really motivates us. He says that the traditional approach of using carrots and sticks to motivate people doesn't work. When it comes to motivation, there's a gap between what science knows and what business does. Our current business operating system (carrot and stick) is ineffectual and often actually does harm.

One of the reasons for this is *The Sawyer Effect* (inspired by the Mark Twain story in which Tom persuades his friends to pay to whitewash a fence). This highlights two crucial effects:

1. **Offering rewards can turn play into work (negative)**

2. **Focusing on mastery can turn work into play (positive)**

In other words, offering incentives is a way to indicate that something is not that interesting to do – thereby immediately reducing the motivation of the person who is being asked to do it. Instead, we need to concentrate on autonomy, mastery and purpose.

- *Autonomy* is the desire to direct our own lives.

- *Mastery* is the urge to get better and better at something that matters.

- *Purpose* is the yearning to do what we do in the service of something larger than ourselves.

These are the three things that motivate us all, and give us our drive. Of course, baseline rewards (salary, contract and a few perks) have to be adequate in order for these atavistic qualities to kick in, and employers have to ensure that those basic needs are met. But beyond that, motivation comes from autonomy, mastery and purpose.

The one-sentence summary
We are driven by autonomy, mastery and purpose – the desire to direct our own lives, get better at something that matters, and be part of something bigger.

He explains two important types of behaviour:

- *Type X behaviour* is based on extrinsic desires such as external rewards.

- *Type I behaviour* is interested in intrinsic rewards – the inherent satisfaction of the activity itself (so long as baseline rewards are adequate).

Employers need to recognise this and understand who they are hiring, and how to motivate them. *'If-then'* rewards usually do more harm than good for creative, conceptual tasks *('If you do this, then you'll get that')*. *'Now that'* rewards are offered after a task has been completed *('Now that you've done such a great job, let's acknowledge the achievement')*, and come as a surprise. These are more effective in the long run, and lead to better motivation.

Low-profit Limited Liability Corporations (L3Cs) are a new breed of company that understands this phenomenon. They operate like a for-profit business and generate a modest profit, but their primary aim is to offer social benefits. They offer high levels of motivation to their employees. For example, the author is a fan of FedEx days (so-called because the staff have a day to get together and have to deliver something new overnight). These allow employees to tackle any problem they want, and are hugely productive. People like *Goldilocks Tasks* best – neither too easy nor too hard. This is where they get 'in the flow' and do their best work. A ROWE is a *Results-Only Work Environment,* where employees don't have schedules. They don't have to be in the office at any particular time; they just have to get their work done.

Understanding what drives people in a more sympathetic and understanding way leads to greater motivation, loyalty and satisfaction. Everyone can win.

CHAPTER 1 WISDOM

- **Geographical boundaries have effectively disappeared where business is concerned.**

- **Turbulence is the new normal – get used to it and develop early-warning systems.**

- **It's the soft things that matter, and they are very hard to do.**

- **We live in a complex world of infinite subtleties and variation – don't try to attribute causality when there is none.**

- **Emotion lies at the heart of consumer behaviour, so it is important to understand exactly how people decide what to buy.**

- **We are driven by autonomy, mastery and purpose – the desire to direct our own lives, get better at something that matters, and be part of something bigger.**

CHAPTER 2.
BEHAVIOURAL ECONOMICS: THE WORLD OF IRRATIONALITY AND CHOICE ARCHITECTURE

Actually, it *is* all about the money

THE UNDERCOVER ECONOMIST, TIM HARFORD

Economists believe that every decision we make can be traced to the power of money. Behavioural Economics says it's more complex than that because people are inherently irrational. The tension between rationality and irrationality makes analysing why people make the decisions they do highly complicated. We'll begin with the economic argument. Tim Harford is the self-styled *Undercover Economist*, and in 2006 he produced a book of the same name. It claims to offer the hidden story behind the forces that shape our everyday lives – it's like spending the day wearing x-ray goggles and suddenly understanding the economic incentive that drives everything.

In theory, economics can illuminate every aspect of the world we inhabit – if it is explained clearly enough. This covers, among other things, why the gap between rich and poor nations is so great, why it's so difficult to get a foot on the property ladder, or why you can't buy a decent second-hand car. Disregarding for a moment the vagaries of human behaviour, it is certainly possible to examine the details of how much people are prepared to spend on what, and to look at the variables that affect purchase decisions. This is the sort of rigor that economists like, because it brings order to an otherwise random world.

Pricing strategy is a case in point. Supermarkets have price targeting down to a fine art. For example, the author bought five products at Marks & Spencer in Liverpool Street station and then walked 500 metres to Moorgate to another M&S store, where pretty much everything was 15 per cent more expensive. This price discrepancy can be viewed in various ways:

1. **Bold and well-informed price variations can be highly effective in increasing margin for companies**

2. **Price variations amount to cynical exploitation of customers.**

3. **Customers are too lazy to walk a few metres to save 15 per cent**

4. **Customers are aware of the differences but don't mind paying the extra**

All these views may be valid, depending on the context. He goes on to show that coffee shops are the same, but then who would walk that distance to save 30p? Price targeting in more expensive consumer durable products goes to much greater extremes. IBM, for example, has to put an additional chip in its low-end printer to slow it down and so justify the lower price. Some would argue that deliberately retarding the performance of a product makes no sense, but this is an example of it being deployed in order to justify the higher price of another model.

Pricing strategies encounter snags when they 'leak' – either when rich customers buy cheap products, or when products leak from one group to another. This is where it can all unravel. As soon as it becomes apparent that a product doesn't need to be expensive, then the whole pack of cards that supports premium pricing can topple. But price targeting is better than group price targeting, which is inefficient because it takes products away from customers who are willing to pay more, and gives them to those who pay less.

The one-sentence summary
Economic incentives drive everything.

Harford suggests that perfectly competitive markets result in four main components:

1. **Companies who make things the right way**
    Everything is produced in the most efficient way, and any company that wastes resources, over-produces or uses the wrong technology will go out of business.

2. **Companies who make the right things**
    The price of a product equals the cost to make it, representing a direct line of communication from what products cost to what customers prefer, and back again.

3. **Things that are made in the right proportions**
    The competitive rule (price = cost = value to the consumer) keeps things efficient, so no one produces less or more than is needed.

4. **Things that are going to the 'right' people**
    The only people buying are the ones willing to pay the appropriate price, so there is no room for any gain in efficiency – you can't get more efficient than a perfectly competitive market.

Of course we all know that there is no such thing as a perfectly competitive market. Some markets suffer from asymmetric information, where one negotiator knows more than the other. With second-hand cars, people won't pay over the odds for one that has a 50/50 chance of being a peach rather than a lemon. Equally, insurance policies are based on mutual ignorance – neither side knows what will happen, so the pricing is effectively made up. Analysing markets and behaviour by pure economics is worthwhile, but it has its limitations.

You don't have to be an expert to understand it

DISCOVER YOUR INNER ECONOMIST, TYLER COWEN

In 2007 Tyler Cowen launched *Discover Your Inner Economist*. Suddenly here was economics for the masses. In what was described as a quirky, incisive romp through everyday life, Cowen applied economic theory to falling in love, surviving your next meeting, motivating your dentist, getting the kids to do the dishes, finding a good guide in a foreign country, and scores of other situations that affect us all. His stance is that anyone can turn economic reasoning to their advantage – at home, work or on holiday. Understanding the incentives that work best with each individual is the key to satisfactory and successful daily interactions, but it only works if we understand the importance of respect for human liberty. Discovering your inner economist can lead to a happier, more satisfying life, he says.

Good economics should adhere to three tests:

1. The Postcard Test

It should always be possible to take a good economics argument and write it on the back of a postcard. If an argument has too many steps, at least one step is bound to be radically uncertain.

2. The Grandma Test

The theory must be intelligible to your grandmother. The other person must at least know what you are talking about.

3. The Aha Principle

If some clearly expressed economic observation is to the point, the thought should be a revelation and invoke the response, 'Aha!'.

To see patterns in human behaviour, we really need to expand our repertoire of recognition chunks. This is effectively a library of recognised patterns that happen time and again. Chess grandmasters can keep 50,000 in their cognitive capacity, and this enables them to project forward and plan scenarios better. Psychologists highlight *Fundamental Attribution Error* or *correspondence bias*. The error is to assume that a single incidence of consumer behaviour represents a deep-rooted personality trait, when in fact it may not. It might just be a result of situational influences. So, for example, we make bad decisions when we are under stress but this is not our 'normal' behaviour, and in reality we are all more typical than we think we are.

The one-sentence summary
Anyone can turn economic reasoning to their own advantage.

Cowen offers three parables:

1. Dirty Dishes

Money doesn't always work: your kids will still not do the washing up if you offer to pay. The failure of the bribe merely reflects the complexity of human motivation.

2. Car Salesman

If you don't pay people, they won't do anything. Hardly anyone sells cars for fun, and car salesmen receive bonuses relating to the number of cars they sell, which is why they bargain so hard.

3. Parking Tickets

People respond to the same incentive in different ways. For example, diplomats from countries with high domestic corruption run up the most parking tickets in New York. The incentive is the same, but the response is different. This last point raises an important consideration: culture can have a deep bearing on reaction to economic incentives, so it is not possible to adopt a one-size-fits-all approach.

A *tragedy of the commons* occurs when individual actions, when taken together, destroy the value of an asset or resource. Common land provides a shared resource for the benefit of all so long as no one abuses it. But as soon as one person does, the whole system collapses. This doesn't just happen in an economic context. For example, in art, has over exposure of the Mona Lisa reduced its intrinsic value to those of us who view the painting? The lines between economic considerations and behavioural traits keep blurring.

When obvious choices aren't obvious

PREDICTABLY IRRATIONAL, DAN ARIELY

Predictably Irrational came out in 2008, sold well, and was immediately revised and expanded a year later. Subtitled *The Hidden Forces that Shape Our Decisions,* the book explains how to break through our systematic patterns of thought to make better, more financially sound, decisions. We think we are in control when it comes to making decisions, but are we? A series of experiments reveal the truth: expectations, emotions, social norms and other invisible, seemingly illogical forces skew our reasoning abilities.

We make astonishingly simple mistakes, and usually the same type:

1. **Consistently overpaying, underestimating and procrastinating**

2. **Failing to understand the effects of emotions on what we want**

3. **Overvaluing what we already own**

The good news is that these misguided behaviours are neither random nor senseless. They're systematic and predictable – hence the title. This book is a close cousin of *Freakonomics, Nudge, Sway* and several other books on Behavioural Economics, the study of the financial implications of the judgements and decisions we make. The promise of the discipline is to learn to take into account our flaws and inabilities when we design our world, and thus make it a better place. And yet its greatest challenge is demonstrating its applicability in the real world.

The one-sentence summary
People are predictably irrational when making decisions, and often make basic mistakes.

The author is a social scientist with a crucial life story that leads to an observational perspective. Aged 18 he was blown up by a magnesium flare in Israel and suffered third-degree burns on 70 per cent of his body. He is therefore one of those people who has more reason than most of us to ponder the meaning of life. He quotes Al Roth, a Harvard economist: *'In theory, there is no difference between theory and practice, but in practice there is a great deal of difference'.* One of the great difficulties with predicting human behaviour and decision-making is that people do some very strange things, despite the attempts of economists to make sense of them.

He suggests various measures that we can grapple with to understand the forces that shape our 'irrational' decision-making behaviour:

1. **Everything is relative: decoy effects fool us into thinking otherwise**
   Providing a third (decoy) option has a huge bearing on what people choose.

2. **Supply and demand links are often a fallacy**
   Beware being imprinted into thinking something is more desirable than it truly is. Sometimes the demand has been artificially created.

3. **Arbitrary coherence is common**
   For example, just thinking about old people can make you walk slower.

4. **Self-herding is habitual behaviour that you create yourself**
   It can make people do daft things, because they often mimic before they work out what they are doing.

5. **The Tom Sawyer principle means that some people will pay you to do something when the transaction should have been the other way round**

   In the story, Tom manages to get his friends to pay him for the privilege of whitewashing his aunt's fence – a task he has been given. (If this sounds familiar, it is the same point as made in the last chapter by Daniel Pink in *Drive*, and a recurring theme with behavioural scientists for decades.)

6. **Free is a confusing concept that makes us go for things we don't really want**

   Not much elaboration required here – just look around your possessions for things that were free and see how much you value them.

7. **You can't mix social and market norms**

   You don't offer to pay for the meal that your mother cooks you. Equally, companies can't have it both ways. If they try to motivate people with cash, it gives the signal that it's work, which doesn't motivate people with Type I characteristics (intrinsic motivation – the inherent satisfaction of the activity itself we saw in the last chapter).

It's complicated stuff, because it doesn't follow a set methodology, and much of the writing is either a synthesis of anecdote, or the drawing together of a series of behavioural experiments. With so much written about Behavioural Economics, perhaps we are spoilt for choice.

So much to choose from, I can't decide...

THE PARADOX OF CHOICE, BARRY SCHWARTZ

Barry Schwartz's book *The Paradox of Choice* came out in 2004, but has enjoyed a renaissance as the Behavioural Economics movement has gained momentum in recent years. Not content with having a subtitle, it has two: *Why more is less,* and *How the culture of abundance robs us of satisfaction.* The author argues that we would be better off if we embraced voluntary constraints and sought what was 'good enough' instead of seeking the best. To reduce stress, we should lower our expectations, make our decisions non-reversible and pay less attention to what others are doing.

Thematically, the book straddles two important areas – the smoldering debate about whether we have over-consumed or not (which we looked at in the last chapter), and the fraught area of choice and decision-making that is the main preoccupation of Behavioural Economics. Schwartz starts from first principles: negative liberty is freedom from (constraint) and positive liberty is freedom to (do what we want). Philosophers the world over have been grappling with this for centuries. The more choice we have, the less we actually make decisions – the tyranny of small decisions paralyses us, and numerous experiments verify this.

Choices are based on expected and remembered utility – how people felt when the experience was at its peak (best or worst) and at the end. The psychologist Daniel Kahneman calls this the *peak-end rule.* Kahneman & Tversky, revered Behavioural Economists, defined the *availability heuristic*, in which people give undue weight to some types of information in relation to others, leading to irrational decisions. As we have seen before, most of us are lousy decision-makers. *Prospect theory* suggests that evaluations are relative to a baseline – a hedonic zero point that determines whether something appears 'better' or 'worse'. These baselines are personal and arbitrary, and do not contribute to rational thought.

Perhaps Schwartz's most famous typology is that of *maximizers* and *satisficers.* Maximizers consider every possibility, are always wondering what the other options are, and are never satisfied. Too much choice increases their stress. Perfectionists set high standards they don't expect to meet, but maximizers do expect to meet them, and are disappointed when they don't. Satisficers (an elided word derived from 'satisfy' and 'suffice') are happy with 'good enough' and have few regrets. To summarise this in the language of the two types:

Satisficer
'I follow the less-is-more approach to making decisions. As long as my choices fit my basic criteria, I'm happy to make decisions with minimal research.'

Maximizer
'I take a much more considered approach, seeking out as much information as possible and exploring all the options before I am confident I've made the right decision.'

The one-sentence summary
The more choice we have, the less we actually make decisions.

So, people who are happy with 'enough' enjoy lower stress levels and increased happiness. On the other hand, there is a state known as *learned helplessness*. This is when a person thinks that it won't work so there's no point in even trying. But assuming we do want to cope better with choice, he offers a number of suggestions:

1. Choose when to choose
Focus time and energy on the decisions that really matter.

2. Be a chooser not a picker
Pickers make relatively passive selections from what's available – choosers concentrate harder.

3. Satisfice more and maximize less
Settling for 'good enough' saves a lot of worry.

4. Think about the opportunity costs of opportunity costs
Ignoring the cost of all the effort that goes into agonising over decisions can lead us to overestimate how good the (apparently) best option is.

5. Make your decisions non-reversible
Being allowed to change our minds increases the chances that we will.

6. Practice an attitude of gratitude
Being thankful for what you've got reduces feelings of jealousy in relation to other options.

7. Regret less
This is a natural consequence of 3, 4 and 6.

8. Anticipate adaptation
The thrill of a new purchase will wane – anticipate this and don't let it upset you.

9. Control expectations

Anchoring affects our expectations, and if we place them too high, we are disappointed.

10. Curtail social comparison

'He who dies with the most toys wins' is just a bumper sticker.

11. Learn to love constraints

Freedom of choice can easily become a tyranny of choice. Work with what you have.

The science of shopping explained

WHY WE BUY, PACO UNDERHILL

Why We Buy is a book with an interesting history. It originally came out in 1999, and was reissued 10 years later, with updated views based on the onset of online shopping. There is a science of shopping, it claims. It can be understood by intense scrutiny of how people behave in the retail environment. The mechanics of shopping shows, among other things, that there is a twilight zone in the entrance of stores that people go straight past; that having two hands restricts their options; that they have real trouble reading signs; that they move in certain clearly defined ways; and that they shift around all the time. Understanding these dynamics and making small changes can lead to massive increases in sales and profits.

People want to see, feel and touch most items they might buy, and yet many store designs, and a lot of packaging, prevents them from doing so. These sensory elements are often ignored in the shopping process. Shopping is defined as experiencing that portion of the world that has been deemed for sale – it is an activity in its own right, not just the acquisition of necessities. The author has developed a confusion index that measures how baffled shoppers are, and an interception rate that measures how often they interact with staff. The *butt-brush factor* determines how closely packed merchandise is – women in particular hate it when people squeeze past them, and it impedes their enjoyment of the shopping experience, even to the point that they may not buy.

Generally speaking, shoppers love touch, mirrors, discovery, talking, recognition and bargains. No major surprises there then. On the other hand, they dislike *too many* mirrors, having to ask dumb questions, dipping down to pick things up, goods being out of stock, obscure price tags and intimidating service. So far, so obvious. Where the science of shopping gets interesting is where small tweaks and details in the retail environment can have an inordinate bearing on sales performance. Examples include:

1. Conversion rate

The CEO who thought his conversion rate was perfect, only to find it was 48 per cent. Changes in layout, display, merchandising and staffing can change this.

2. Time in store

A storeowner thinks people spend 10 minutes in store, when in fact it is two. Similar measures can be applied.

3. Convenience

Giving people a basket when their hands are full means they will buy more.

4. Opportunity to try

Sixty-five per cent of men who try something on buy it, but only 25 per cent of women do the same. The dressing room is the most important room in a store, but has the least investment.

5. Waiting time

Perception of waiting time can be 'bent' by human interaction, orderliness of queuing, companionship and diversion – these make people wait longer more happily.

The one-sentence summary
Small changes to the shopping experience can make a huge difference to sales.

The subject matter of this book is where the somewhat abstract area of Behavioural Economics meets the gritty reality of the retail environment. Theory is nothing without application in real circumstances. The book was never written as a specific contribution to the Behavioural Economics debate, but a decade later it has unwittingly become so. This may well be because the theory is always looking for practical circumstances to offer as proof. Over 10 years after it was written, it is interesting to see how the thinking applies to the newly created world of online shopping. Perhaps not surprisingly, the author makes it clear that he is not a fan of online shopping, and says so at some length. Whether this means that his views are less relevant now is up to the reader to decide.

Your brain knows more than you do

BUYOLOGY, MARTIN LINDSTROM

Subtitled *How Everything We Believe About Why We Buy is Wrong,* the book tries to explain why we don't always buy things for the reasons we think we do. It uses neuromarketing, an intriguing marriage of marketing and science, to provide a window into the human mind. *Buyology* (2008) is defined as the subconscious thoughts, feelings, and desires that drive purchasing decisions. Lindstrom's main point is that conventional research doesn't work to explain these decisions. Neither quantitative surveys nor qualitative groups correlate well with actual sales. As a general point, we are a lot better at collecting data than doing anything useful with it.

His investigations are mildly controversial because they involve hooking respondents up to a range of wires or putting them in scanners. Not everyone approves of the research techniques because they feel too close to lab experiments. The two main techniques are SST (Steady State Topography) and FMRI (Functional Magnetic Resonance Imaging). They effectively show which parts of the brain react to various stimuli. His belief is that by understanding better our seemingly irrational behaviour we can gain more control of our actions.

The one-sentence summary
People don't always buy things for the reasons they think they do.

Lindstrom's techniques reveal some interesting things, including which marketing approaches do and don't work, according to what our brain patterns are revealing:

1. Product placement·doesn't work

Even though many companies spend a fortune doing it. We just don't remember enough to do anything about it.

2. Sex doesn't work

Sex detracts from decent branding. This is the *Vampire Effect* – sucking attention away from what ads are actually trying to say.

3. Shock tactics don't work

Warnings about the perils of smoking can increase smoking because they unintentionally trigger all the (nice) cues that people associate with it.

4. Subliminal messages work

This is why people want to smoke more when in a Marlboro lounge containing imagery subtly reminiscent of the brand.

5. Rituals work

As in the 119.53 seconds it takes to pour a pint of Guinness.

6. Faith and religion work

Strong brands excite the brain in the same way as religious images.

7. Somatic markers work

These are the shortcuts that your brain makes to associate memories with brands.

8. Mirror neurons work

They make us imitate the actions we observe, which is why crazes and marketing phenomena catch on via copying.

Twelve billion dollars is spent on market research in the United States every year, and yet eight out of 10 new products fail within the first three months, so it doesn't really work. This isn't particularly supposed to be a condemnation of the market research industry, although it is hard to conclude otherwise in the face of this data. For example, the Pepsi Challenge misled marketers because it was a sip test. When people drink a whole can, Coke still wins. All of which may mean that the brain can fool its owner and market researchers at the same time. But is endless choice really endless?

Oh dear, we've run out of steam

THE GREAT STAGNATION, TYLER COWEN

Consumer choice relies on spending power and plenty of products to choose from. But actually, we are in the middle of *The Great Stagnation,* according to Tyler Cowen. The snappy subtitle of this 2011 e-book is *How America Ate All the Low-Hanging Fruit of Modern History, Got Sick, and Will (Eventually) Recover.* The overall line of argument is that most of the things that generated economic growth have now been used up (the low-hanging fruit), certainly from a US perspective. We need to get used to this to have a more realistic view of how economies can work and what they can afford. The *LHF* that America 'ate' was all the free land, the quantity of technological breakthroughs and improved education that fuelled growth. This lasted about 300 years but has now mostly gone.

Most developed countries have seen their economic growth slowing since the 1970s because technological development has slowed. It was easier for the average person to produce an important innovation in the nineteenth century than in the twentieth. This means a lower and declining rate of return on technology. A lot of our recent innovations are 'private goods' rather than 'public goods' – they have made a few individuals very wealthy but do not translate into gains for the average citizen.

The one-sentence summary
We have used up most of the breakthroughs that fuelled growth, so stagnation and less choice is the new normal.

The theory is interesting: when you combine three macroeconomic events – growing income inequality, stagnant median income and the financial crisis – you can see why our 'new economy' is not as productive as before. Productivity figures that rise can be misleading. For example, the biggest gain in the last few years has been discovering who *isn't* producing very much, and then firing them. Although the Internet is highly innovative, it doesn't generate nearly as many jobs or as much income as traditional businesses. Google has 20,000 employees and eBay 16,400, but Facebook has only 1,700 and Twitter 300. The Internet is great because it gives us 'cheap fun' but it's not generating the scale of revenue necessary to replace what we've lost. Cowen's recommendation is to raise the social status of scientists, so that we fuel more ideas that generate growth. Other than that, 'we are living in the new normal', and that means less choice.

CHAPTER 2 WISDOM

- **Economic incentives drive everything.**

- **Anyone can turn economic reasoning to their own advantage.**

- **People are predictably irrational when making decisions, and often make basic mistakes.**

- **The more choice we have, the less we actually make decisions.**

- **Small changes to the shopping experience can make a huge difference to sales.**

- **People don't always buy things for the reasons they think they do.**

- **We have used up most of the breakthroughs that fuelled growth, so stagnation and less choice is the new normal.**

CHAPTER 3. ORGANISATIONAL THEORY: LIVE COMPANIES AND DEAD ISSUES

Your boss may be dead boring, but the company lives

THE LIVING COMPANY, ARIE DE GEUS

What if we thought about a company as a living being, rather than just a series of monetary assets? This is the question posed by Arie de Geus in 1997. He spent most of his career at Shell, and is widely credited with originating the concept of the learning organisation – how to create growth, learning and longevity in business. Setting up companies would appear to be reasonably easy but keeping them going is harder.

Seeing a company as a machine implies that it is fixed, that it will eventually run down, and that its people are straightforward (human) resources. Living companies evolve naturally because people generate change, they regenerate of their own accord and can learn as entities. The average company lifespan is 40 years, with humans lasting 70. Companies tend to die early because the thinking and language of management are too narrowly based on economics. They forget that their organisation's true nature is that of a community of humans. His research shows that long-lived companies have four important components:

1. **Learning**
   Sensitivity to their environment and an ability to learn and adapt.

2. **Persona**
   Cohesion and a strong sense of identity, with an innate ability to build a community.

3. Ecology
Tolerance, decentralisation and an ability to build relationships with other entities.

4. Evolution
An ability to govern their own growth effectively, including conservative finance.

The one-sentence summary
Companies are living entities that thrive by learning, having a strong persona, and governing their growth efficiently.

The Swedish neurobiologist David Ingvar describes a 'memory of the future', in which we have envisaged a series of scenarios. Usually 60 per cent are positive and 40 per cent negative, but if the balance is disturbed then incorrigible optimists or pessimists take centre stage. This can have a huge bearing on the fortunes of companies, depending on who is in charge and the nature of their prevailing view. There are lots of theories about the possible reasons why managers so often fail. These include:

1. Managers are stupid
De Geus does not believe this. The biggest problem is not that individuals act unintelligently in isolation but that overall, companies fail to pool their collective intelligence to foresee problems together.

2. We can only see when a crisis opens our eyes
People don't like change, but some quite enjoy a crisis. At least then it is possible to *do* something.

3. **We can only see what we have already experienced**
   This may not be true – both new and old companies
   often miss the signals that denote impending crises.

4. **We cannot see what is emotionally difficult to see**
   Emotional pain accompanies almost every tough
   decision, so many managers avoid them.

5. **We can only see what is relevant to our view of the future**
   In Ingvar's scheme, our memory of the future prepares
   us for action, but also acts as a filter to help deal with
   information overload.

Few companies are as capable as human beings at dealing
with the future. Managers see signals of a potential future,
but still don't necessarily respond in a timely fashion to that
future, even after it has occurred. In the 1930s the corporate world tried to address this with 'tools for foresight' – the
dreaded strategic planning that creates the illusion of certainty where there is none.

But in truth most companies learn through perceiving,
embedding, concluding and acting:

1. **Perceiving**
   This usually involves someone calling a meeting
   because something has happened. Someone develops a
   mental model or interpretation of what is happening.

2. **Embedding**
   Then people spend most of their time explaining to
   each other how they see the problem. People
   externalise and calibrate their mental models.

3. Concluding

Plans are drawn up, along with 'what if?' scenarios.

4. Acting

Something is done, and usually it is monitored and tracked. Then it all starts again.

In this respect, all decision-making is a learning activity, but it can take a long time for the knowledge to be assimilated, and it may not reside with the company if managers move on too often. It can also be slow, and lead to the closing down of options if things are always done the same way. So much for viewing an organisation as a living, breathing entity, but what if it's not?

Most conventional ways of working are rubbish

REWORK, FRIED & HANSSON

Most of what you are told about building, running and growing a business is nonsense, according to Jason Fried and David Heinemeier Hansson in *Rework* (2010). You can change the way you work forever by ignoring most conventions from normal companies, they say. This is the kind of book that fights the anti-establishment corner with pithy aphorisms such as ASAP is poison, underdo the competition, meetings are toxic, fire the workaholics, and many more. It doesn't really have conventional chapters. Instead it has ultra-short sections with punchy pieces of advice. There are lots of them, over 80 in fact, and so too many to list in full, but they include:

1. **Ignore the real world**
   People who say something won't work are often wrong.

2. **Learning from mistakes is overrated**
   Learn from your successes, not your failures.

3. **Planning is guessing**
   Have a go and get on with it.

4. **Why grow?**
   Being a large business may be pointless and counterproductive.

5. **Workaholism is for fools**
   You don't have to be that busy to succeed.

6. **Enough with 'entrepreneurs'**
   Let's just call them starters.

7. **Make a dent in the universe**
   Try to change something.

8. **Scratch your own itch**
   Do something you want to do.

9. **Start making something**
   No time is no excuse.

10. **Outside money is plan Z**
    Don't borrow if you don't have to.

11. **Embrace constraints**
    They make your work more specific.

12. **Throw less at the problem**
    Do less, better.

13. Sell your by-products
The stuff you reject on the way may have value too.

14. Meetings are toxic
Have as few as possible.

15. Good enough is fine
Get something underway and fix it as you go.

16. Long lists don't get done
Make tiny decisions and see the progress.

17. Don't confuse enthusiasm with priority
The enthusiasm you have for a new idea is not an indicator of its true worth.

The one-sentence summary
Ignore what normal companies do and do the opposite.

The gems keep coming: inspiration is perishable, fight bloat and throw less at the problem. You could dip into this book anywhere and grab a motivating thought on anything from launching to hiring, productivity to promotion. It is brilliantly contrary, and is most likely to generate cheers of approval from mavericks everywhere, and howls of protest from traditional corporate citizens. It is probably easier to apply some of this to smaller gangs of people, but what happens if you need to co-ordinate hundreds or thousands of them?

Animals are better organised than we are

SMART SWARM, PETER MILLER

Organisations are notoriously dysfunctional, and if you want to know how to solve the problem, ask some termites. *National Geographic* senior editor Peter Miller sets us straight in *Smart Swarm* (2010), showing how animal colonies are so much better organised than we can ever be. He aims to show that understanding how flocks, schools and colonies work can make us better at communicating, decision-making and getting things done. Studying the collective intelligence of ants, bees, termites, birds, fish and locusts can give us great ideas for solving business and social problems. Many of them have already been adopted by the worlds of finance, the military and even Google.

The major principles of a smart swarm are:

1. **Self-organisation**
   This is made up of decentralised control (nobody's in charge); distributed problem-solving (each individual sorts something out); and multiple interactions (lots of individuals paying attention to what the other is doing).

2. **Diversity of knowledge**
   When many bees head in different directions looking for honey, they increase the hive's collective chance of finding it. It's a probability game with good communication when a decent source has been found.

3. **Indirect collaboration**
   In a process sometimes called *stigmergy,* termites follow a simple rule of 'drop your grain of sand here if somebody else has already done so'. The collaboration

is indirect because they do not have to interact with a colleague for this to occur, and the communication is achieved indirectly by modifying the environment.

4. Adaptive mimicking
Coordination, communication and copying can unleash powerful waves of energy in a collective population. An example would be when the wall of a termite mound is breached and it needs urgent repair.

As is so often the case with books of this type, enigmatic questions are posed on the cover. These include, How can bees help run board meetings? How can ant colonies make flying stress-free? and How can fish fight terrorism? The answers lie of course in the inner workings and intricate group behaviour of the various colonies, whose ability to organise, 'systemitise' and problem-solve frequently makes our collective efforts look rather pathetic. As the old saying goes, there is intelligent life on earth, but it's not necessarily us.

The one-sentence summary
Understanding flocks, schools and colonies can make us better at communicating, decision-making and getting things done.

Swarm lessons can be salutary in helping companies, but it does require the individual to subsume their own ambition or self-interest for the benefit of the whole. So for example:

1. Seek a diversity of knowledge
As many people as possible should be encouraged to draw from diverse sources, like many bees looking for honey.

2. **Encourage a friendly competition of ideas**
   The more options, the greater the likelihood of a winning answer to a problem. All the best suggestions can then be analysed on their merits.

3. **Use an effective mechanism to narrow your choices**
   The strength of support given to a bee's waggle dance may indicate the best location for a new hive.

4. **Amplifying success**
   The more ants take the shortest path, the more continue to do so, thus increasing efficiency. This can be emulated in the business world by replicating shortcuts and most effective routes to get things done.

Many businesses are like a complex adaptive organism without a central nervous system, with units operating in silos and not sharing knowledge, which is clearly not beneficial for the whole. It is proven that groups of three or four people perform better than the best individual on their own because their sum total of problem-solving skills is greater, so it would help companies perform better if they worked more like smart swarms.

Intelligent people are very hard to deal with

CLEVER, GOFFEE & JONES

Rob Goffee and Gareth Jones know a lot about how companies work, and in 2009 they grappled with a particularly thorny issue: how to lead your smartest, most clever people. Research shows that a handful of star performers create disproportionate amounts of value for their organisations, but they argue that you need a particularly astute approach to lead smart, creative people because they can be a bit of a pain to handle. On first examination, you might think that these people could be free agents who may be more successful working for themselves, but that is not actually the case. In fact, they need their organisation's commercial and financial resources to fulfill their potential, albeit in a slightly less conventional way than the average employee.

The authors call these invaluable individuals *clevers* – they can be brilliant, difficult and sometimes even dangerous, and success may well depend on how well they are led, which is a nightmare in itself. They identify *value rationality* – a logic of goals and ends that occur when a company has an aspirational cause. This is an interdependence of equals. The characteristics of *clevers* are many and varied: their cleverness is central to their identity; their skills are not easily replicated; they know their worth; they ask difficult questions; they are organisationally savvy; they are not impressed by hierarchy; they expect instant success; they want to be connected to other clever people; and they won't thank you. It's a charming list to handle if you are in charge of these people. Traditional leadership approaches won't be effective. Instead, Goffee & Jones offer specific advice for bosses who have to deal with these types:

1. Tell them what – but not how

A sense of direction is helpful, but don't tell them *how* to do things, because they like to work it out for themselves.

2. Provide boundaries

They need 'organised space' for their creativity.

3. **Earn their respect with expertise, not a job title**
   Clevers don't expect their bosses to know everything they do, but they do expect them to be an expert in their own field.

4. **Sense their needs and keep them motivated**
   Listening to the silences helps to anticipate their frustrations.

5. **Shelter them from administrative and political distractions**
   This 'organisational rain' is highly distracting and is not something they can usefully be involved with.

6. **Connect them with clever peers**
   The role of the leader is to conduct and connect – as a compass to direct; as a magnet to attract the talent; and as a bridge to bring the *clevers* together.

7. **Convince them the company can help them succeed**
   This is the higher goal that persuades them that they are in the right place to realise their ambitions.

It all adds up to leading with a confident, light touch, explaining and persuading, using expertise and giving space and resources. Getting the approach right works for individuals, teams and even whole companies, because *clevers* attract more *clevers*.

The one-sentence summary

A handful of clever star performers create disproportionate amounts of value for organisations, but they must be managed particularly astutely.

Of course, it goes without saying that these *clevers* have a rap sheet of bad characteristics. These include:

1. **taking pleasure in breaking the rules;**

2. **trivialising the importance of non-technical people;**

3. **being oversensitive about their projects;**

4. **suffering from knowledge-is-power syndrome;**

5. **never being happy about the review process.**

It's a nasty list, and one that could strike fear into the heart of anyone who has to deal with creative people. Strangely though, the idea of enjoying breaking the rules, ridiculing those less intelligent, being defensive, and generally gainsaying the ways of the company may not be any more counter-cultural than the way many staff behave most of the time as a matter of course. It's just that when that behaviour manifests itself in someone whose contribution really matters to the fortunes of the company, it probably gets noticed more.

Forget words and try a big chart

BUSINESS MODEL GENERATION, OSTERWALDER &
PIGNEUR
This book claims to be a handbook for visionaries, game changers, and challengers striving to defy outmoded business models and design tomorrow's enterprises. No pressure there then. It was 'co-created' in 2010 by 470 strategy practitioners from 45 countries, and provides a rallying call to change the way you think about business models.

The book started life as a work-in-progress idea and was developed independently of the traditional publishing industry, which means that the method in it has been test-driven many times already. It is a highly visual method, which shows a system moving in a sequence, the main theme of which is the canvas, which has nine building blocks that are constantly reworked throughout. All the segments interlock to form a one-page view of your particular business model. The elements are:

1. **Customer segments**
   Which customer(s) does your organisation serve?

2. **Value propositions**
   Which customer needs do you satisfy, or what problems do you solve?

3. **Channels**
   Which communication, distribution or sales channels do you use?

4. **Customer relationships**
   How are these established and maintained with each segment?

5. **Revenue streams**
   Resulting from which value propositions to which customers?

6. **Key resources**
   Which assets are required to offer and deliver all the above?

7. **Key activities**
   What needs to be done?

8. Key partnerships

Do any activities or resources need to be outsourced or acquired?

9. Cost structure

What are the most important costs, and which are the most expensive?

A canvas can be started with any of these elements, and when they are all in place, it enables you to look at an existing business from many different perspectives, or design an entirely new one. A variety of patterns are shown, from the Long Tail, to free, open, and multi-sided platforms. The permutations are effectively endless. There are then a series of design systems, prototyping and scenario techniques to move from plan to reality, evaluate strategy, design a process, and bring everything to fruition.

The one-sentence summary
Mapping out a visual canvas of a business model helps you to understand, design, test and implement it more easily than with words alone.

The book is presented in a pleasing landscape shape that enables you to view your plans as proper canvases. These are meticulously designed so that you can compare lots of different spreads to view the shape of a business, then draw up your own by running sessions with colleagues and covering them with infinitely changeable sticky notes. You are almost certain to find a fresh perspective here by analysing your business, or a proposed new one, in hundreds of different ways. The approach is mainly visual, so you don't need to wade through many words to come up with a practical exercise for a planning session. Of course, the language of business models is always in danger of straying into cliché, so your decisions on whether an idea has merit or not should always be screened with a bullshit test.

Stop making excuses and get on with it

DO THE WORK, STEVEN PRESSFIELD

In 2011 Seth Godin set up The Domino Project, a joint venture with Amazon designed to short-circuit conventional publishing techniques and get e-books out fast. Apart from launching his own effort *Poke the Box* (see Chapter 5), his first production was by Steven Pressman. Entitled *Do The Work,* it echoed one of Godin's obsessions – that the real skill in life is to 'ship', that is to produce something and get it out into the public domain. Everything else is just (in Godin's words) hobbyism and fiddling about at the edges. Not surprising then that he sympathised with the sentiments of Pressman, who asserts that, '*if you have something to do, then you should get on with it*'. So far, so unoriginal, since we have read scores of books exhorting us to do just that, when we know it is far easier said than done.

Deeper levels of interest are, however, lurking soon after. The great enemies of getting things done are resistance, rational thought and friends and family. Resistance itself includes fear, self-doubt, procrastination, addiction, distraction, timidity, ego, self-loathing, narcissism and much more. It's a daunting list that would put most people off doing anything, ever. The resistance to which he is referring applies to anything you feel you want to do: anything creative, the launch of a venture, a diet or health regime, education, any act of political or moral courage – anything that rejects immediate gratification in favour of long-term growth, health or integrity.

But it's not all bad news. Allies in doing the work are stupidity, stubbornness, blind faith, passion, assistance and friends and family (they can be both good and bad). You have to be dogged (or stupid) enough to carry on, and irrational passion for something is a great help, although it may drive everyone else nuts. The knack is to start *before* you are ready – don't over-prepare or research, just start. Ideally, start at the end and ask yourself: what's all this about? Keep hacking away until you've got something, and then don't sit on it wondering what people will think; take a deep breath and ship it. It takes balls of steel to ship – to send out the result of what you have laboured to do.

The one-sentence summary
Getting things done involves doggedly overcoming resistance, and having the courage to ship your product.

Organisational advice applies equally to individuals as it does to companies. Everyone needs help getting things done. Pressman advises us to stay primitive (the dafter it sounds, the better it probably is), trust the soup (let go of control and trust the Quantum Soup), and be ready for the dreaded resistance. Being able to overcome this is in part linked to coping with the wall, which is what you hit when you can't advance any further. He proposes seven principles to help you do the work:

1. **There is an enemy**
   Admit it.

2. **The enemy is implacable**
   Its aim is to kill what you are doing.

3. **The enemy is inside you**
   It's no good blaming anyone else.

4. **You retain the free will to resist it**
   You need to exercise that choice.

5. **The real you must duel the resistance you**
   Fight the demons in your head.

6. **Resistance arises second**
   You get a great idea, then resistance tries to neuter
   your dream or plan.

7. **Assistance can beat resistance**
   How bad do you want it?

So there you have it. Any company or individual can get
things done effectively if it faces up strongly to resistance.
As with so much business advice, it's up to you.

It's all quite simple if you follow the rules

THE RULES OF MANAGEMENT, RICHARD TEMPLAR
Described as a definitive code for managerial success, this
book provides 100 rules — a blend of serious advice tinged
with a fair dollop of cynicism. The author has apparently
cornered the market in writing the rules, since this 2005
book is the sister title to at least three others, covering
the rules of work, wealth and even life. *The Rules*

of Management is divided into managing your team and managing yourself, and perhaps, tellingly, 34 rules are devoted to the team, and a whopping 66 to oneself. Managing your team points include:

1. **Get them emotionally involved**
   Many manage aloofly.

2. **Set realistic targets**
   How often does that happen?

3. **Hold effective meetings**
   When were you last in one of these?

4. **Offload as much as you can, or dare**
   Master the art of delegation.

5. **Be ready to prune**
   This is the tough bit.

6. **Take the rap**
   This is even tougher.

7. **Be ready to say 'yes'**
   Of course others would say that saying 'no' is equally important.

Managing yourself points include:

1. **Have a game plan, but keep it secret**
   A bit odd this – most would publicise it.

2. **Be consistent**
   How many managers change their minds all the time?

3. Get rid of superfluous rules

Slightly ironic in a book that offers 100 of them?

4. Learn from your mistakes

Repeating the same ineffective stuff gets you nowhere.

5. Manage your health

Do you have a stressed-out boss?

6. Don't stagnate

Hanging frantically on to a job is bad for all.

The one-sentence summary

You can succeed by paying close attention to how you manage yourself and others.

It is full of inspirational quotes:

'Getting good players is easy. Getting them to play together is the hard part.'
Casey Stengel, New York Yankees manager

'The ideas that come out of brainstorming sessions are usually superficial, trivial, and not very original. They are rarely useful. The process, however, seems to make uncreative people feel that they are making innovative contributions and that others are listening to them.'
A. Harvey Block

'It is amazing how much you can accomplish if you do not care who gets the credit.'
Harry Truman

'It's a very difficult job and the only way through is that we all work together as a team. And that means you do everything I say.'
Michael Caine, in *The Italian Job*

You can immediately see the potential conflict between being a wonderful person and being an effective boss. Arguably, no book has ever resolved this. Managing effectively involves three choices: put up with it, change it or end it. As ever, it is usually easier to suggest these things than actually enact them.

CHAPTER 3 WISDOM

- Companies are living entities that thrive by learning, having a strong persona, and governing their growth efficiently.

- Ignore what normal companies do and do the opposite.

- Understanding flocks, schools and colonies can make us better at communicating, decision-making and getting things done.

- A handful of clever star performers create disproportionate amounts of value for organisations, but they must be managed particularly astutely.

- Mapping out a visual canvas of a business model helps you to understand, design, test and implement it more easily than with words alone.

- Getting things done involves doggedly overcoming resistance, and having the courage to ship your product.

- You can succeed by paying close attention to how you manage yourself and others.

CHAPTER 4.
TRENDS AND MOODS: THINGS GO UP AND DOWN

Times are crazy but you can still thrive

REVOLUTION, BILL LUCAS

To survive our current crazy world we need a new kind of *mind-ware* – ways to develop our adaptive intelligence, according to Bill Lucas in 2009's *Revolution*. In a cunning typographical twist, the cover reads *rEvolution*. One hundred and fifty years after Charles Darwin invented the concept of natural selection, the rules of evolution are changing, he says, with the speed of change accelerating faster than ever. *Mind-ware* consists of personal habits of mind and patterns of social interaction, and these need to evolve constantly in order for us to cope with changing times.

In particular, we all need to become better at dealing with absurd amounts of information. Too much choice makes us unhappy, as we have seen with the paradox of choice. Learners inherit the earth, while the learned are beautifully equipped to deal with a world that no longer exists. It's a salutary lesson. We need to explore the unlearning curve: how quickly can we unlearn what we know? This is a tricky business, and definitely easier said than done for those of us set in our ways. How we see the world depends on:

1. **Permanence**
   Pessimists think it's fixed, and optimists move on.

2. **Personalisation**
   Pessimists blame themselves, and optimists get round things.

3. **Pervasiveness**
   Pessimists let setbacks spread, and optimists see isolated incidents.

Coping with change involves adopting new approaches. Visible thinking encourages a tangible response to new stimuli: what's going on here and what do I see that makes me say so? Careful thought around those two questions leads to a more adaptive approach. Unfreeze/move/ refreeze summarises the change process, and Lucas rightly observes that it's not the changes that do you in, it's the transitions. Many of us, and companies, can get from A to B. It's the journey that hurts.

The one-sentence summary
We need to unlearn and learn constantly to keep adapting to an ever-changing world.

He proposes nine rules to work with:

1. **Change is changing**
   It is no longer gradual. We need to cultivate habits of mind associated with imagining, noticing, choosing, synthesising and unlearning.

2. **Real change is internal**
   Instead of looking at the outside world, we should look to letting go, noticing and naming emotions, and the development of resilience.

3. **Slow down**
   Being, deferring, surfacing and reflecting are helpful qualities here.

4. **We can all change the way we see the world**
   Personality and events are not fixed and inevitable.

5. **We can learn how to change more effectively**
   Adaptive intelligence holds the key.

6. **No one can make you change**
   We don't have to follow the herd.

7. **Sometimes it's smart to resist**
   Not all change is helpful.

8. **Use the brainpower of those around you**
   Sociability and working together help tremendously.

9. **Make up your own rules**
   Find your own style and go with it.

This is a generous compendium of practical ideas that any of us can grab and apply to our lives. The PDSA cycle is crucial here: *plan, do, study, act.* This was widely popularised by W. Edwards Deming, the guru of the quality improvement movement. When we notice that something is not working properly, we should *plan* a small intervention to improve things. The new system should be tried out for a short period *(do)*, and the difference should be measured *(study)*. You then *act* differently in the light of what is found out. The study element is crucial, and one can immediately see that many companies short-circuit the process and just opt for a plan/do approach that may or may not work.

Classifying things is a nightmare

EVERYTHING IS MISCELLANEOUS, DAVID WEINBERGER
If the world has gone a bit nuts, the sheer volume of information we have to cope with plays a large part, along with our approach to the Internet that carries a huge proportion

of it. *Everything is Miscellaneous,* according to David Weinberger (2007), and the rules of the physical world (in which everything has its place) have been upended as business, politics, science and media move online. In the digital world everything has its places (plural), with transformative effects, and this is part of the power of the new digital disorder. These effects include:

1. **Information is now a social asset**
   It should be made available for anyone to link, organise and make more valuable.

2. **There's no such thing as 'too much' information**
   It gives people the hooks to find what they need.

3. **Messiness is a digital virtue**
   This leads to new ideas, efficiency and social knowledge.

4. **Authorities are less important than buddies**
   If you want trustworthy information, you're more likely to get it from friends.

The one-sentence summary
The rules of the physical world do not apply online: everything is now miscellaneous.

Physical space puts some things nearer than others. Objects can only be in one spot at a time. There is only one layout and things need to be neat otherwise you struggle to find them. Information isn't like that – it doesn't just want to be free, it wants to be miscellaneous. That means you might find it in multiple places, and access it from all sorts of different angles.

Atoms take up room, but content is digitised into bits. This is the 'third order' that removes the limitations on how we organise information. The first order is the physical items themselves, and the second is metadata (information about information – our systems for organising things). We have many ways to do this: nesting includes *trees* (such as genealogy) and *maps* (in which *lumps* are units of land, and *splits* are the arbitrary divisions between them). These days we need a *faceted classification* system that dynamically constructs a browsable, branching tree that exactly meets our needs. And you thought you simply searched something on your computer and it all just happened. The author believes that the new principles of organising information are:

1. **Filter on the way out, not on the way in**
   Let the user decide how and where they want to access information.

2. **Put each leaf (of data) on as many branches as possible**
   This will increase the chances of people finding what they want.

3. **Everything is metadata and everything can be a label**
   Whether it's a date, a number, a word, it's all classifiable.

4. **Give up control**
   Let data become '*intertwingled*'. The term intertwingularity was invented by Ted Nelson, the eccentric visionary who also coined the term *hypertext* in the mid-1960s.

This last point could be frustrating, but is probably genius. Nelson stated that people keep pretending that they can make things deeply hierarchical, categorisable, and sequential when in fact they can't. Many companies and individuals crave order, but it may not get them anywhere. An article on Wikipedia is deemed 'neutral' when people have stopped changing it (NPOV means No Point Of View), but life is messier than that. Online recommendations can come horribly unstuck when they look to categorise too much. Amazon is easily capable of recommending books on adoption for those looking at abortion. So the message of the book works in two directions. If you are placing something online, make sure it can be searched and accessed from multiple directions. And if you are looking for something, you need to hope that the originator thought the same way.

Trust a company? You're joking...

BAD SCIENCE, BEN GOLDACRE

Bad Science (2008) purports to dispense fast and powerful relief from scaremongering journalists, flaky statistics and evil pharmaceutical corporations. The author dismantles the claims of foolish quacks, via the credence they are given in the mainstream media, and the tricks of the food supplements industry. Scientists and doctors, he claims, are outnumbered and outgunned by vast armies of individuals who feel entitled to pass judgement on matters of evidence without obtaining a basic understanding of the issues.

So here we have a classic collision between a highly sceptical writer, big corporations, and industry commentators, in many cases self-appointed. Stories are often the basis of scientific and medical reporting, but as he rightly points out, the plural of anecdote is not data. Few public examples bear relation to the true issues. People are more likely to listen to advice when they have paid for it, so studies verify that the more expensive something is, the more effective it is perceived to be. Things can happen at the same time, but that is weak, circumstantial evidence for causation. Is it a surprise that those who stand to benefit most financially from the success of something promote its value the most?

When an honest person speaks, they say only what they believe to be true (liars do the opposite, of course). Bullshitters are on neither side. They don't care if they describe reality correctly, so long as they can get away with whatever suits their purpose – usually financial gain. The 'opportunity cost' of this is vast. Cargo-cult science surrounds itself with all the paraphernalia of science without truly having any. This is based on the cargo cults in the war who saw planes landing with many of the things they desired, and subsequently set up landing strips, wore headphones and antennae made of wood, and waited for more planes. None came.

The one-sentence summary
Numbers can ruin lives. They are repeatedly misused and misunderstood, so make sure you understand your data properly.

PR agencies collude with journalists to generate articles that carry more weight than advertising, or replace it if advertising is not allowed. This also circumnavigates tough restrictions on what can be claimed on packaging, because journalism isn't subject to such rules. The real purpose of the scientific method is to make sure nature hasn't misled you into thinking you know something you actually don't know, but clever people believe stupid things when it is presented in a 'sciencey' way. Numbers can ruin lives. They are repeatedly misused and misunderstood. This is unfortunate in journalism, but can be (literally) fatal in medicine.

This book is mainly dedicated to science claims, but it has much broader implications. It is not a textbook. You need to use the medical and scientific points and apply them in a business context, because they are analogous. So many times in business we see data being presented as though it is fact. Often, closer analysis reveals it is nothing of the sort. We regularly see large corporations exposed for nefarious moneymaking techniques. This needs to be watched constantly. And there are fewer more emotive subjects than health, because it really does affect us all personally. The author is a prolific blogger, and is constantly railing against pill-pushing nutritionists and incomprehensible government proposals. The lessons for all are pretty straightforward: don't always believe what you read, and if you are going to take action based on information, make sure you have delved deeply to make sure it is authentic.

Accurate prediction is possible, but companies still get it wrong

PREDICTING MARKET SUCCESS, ROBERT PASSIKOFF
So much for the big stuff. Now let's dive into the details of how on earth someone running a brand can work out whether a marketing initiative is going to be a success or not. It sounds straightforward enough but it clearly isn't, otherwise there wouldn't be so many failures. *Predicting Market Success* (2006) claims that you can explain why

people buy certain things from certain companies, even though other products from other companies seem just as good. He believes that loyalty is the main component of brand strength, and he knows how to measure it accurately.

Brand success is the degree to which the brand meets or exceeds what consumers want, need and expect in the category, both emotionally and rationally. Brands that do this have equity. Brands that don't have problems. The technique the book explains is to evaluate brands (what already exists in the present) against the ideal (what consumers wish existed in the future). This generates a consumer-centric view of the category in which the brand competes, letting it understand how consumers view, compare, and choose among category options. As such this is a predictive solution rather than a historical one. It can easily be integrated into current research efforts, and can demonstrate Brand Equity Return On Investment, quantifying the impact of marketing initiatives *in advance* of spend.

This is effectively a loyalty-based customer listening system that claims to outperform traditional research methods. Today's purchasing decisions are 70 per cent emotional, so there's a big difference between what consumers say they want and what they end up buying. As such, the old model of product, place, price and promotion has been replaced with customer engagement, expectations and loyalty.

The one-sentence summary
Ignore important-sounding but resonance-free offerings and concentrate on bridging the gap between what you deliver and what consumers want.

Research tells you little until you examine the category drivers, their vital components, their order of importance, what expectations people have of them, and how your brand stacks up against all of these. Even worse, they are changing all the time and need to be measured regularly. Then you can plot your brand against category expectations and quantify the gap between what people want and what your brand is actually delivering. For example, your brand rating could go up, but category expectations might go up even further, thus increasing the gap. Looking only at the former figure will provide false optimism for the brand owner, and lead to falling sales.

Consumer expectations are up 28 per cent on average so keeping pace with what they really want is crucial, and yet 85 per cent of new products fail. People knowing a brand (awareness), or even loving it (admiration), is not the same as using it (purchase). Measuring the wrong part is misleading. Plenty of companies use 'important-sounding but resonance-free' offerings as a basis for brand success. But it doesn't generate success, because it so often fails to bridge the gap between what is on offer and what customer expectations truly are. And in fast-moving markets, it doesn't take long for such gaps to appear.

Many marketers come unstuck because they prefer a hunch and a supposedly big idea to detailed statistical analysis and what can sometimes be a rather dry picking over of the numbers. They may also lack the patience to put in place truly robust, valuable surveys and wait for reliable long-term data to come in. But such a rigorous approach reaps its rewards. However, beware if graphs scare you, because there are lots of them here.

Where modern companies are heading

CREATIVE DISRUPTION, SIMON WALDMAN

Many traditional businesses have been caught napping by the onset of the online phenomenon, and as Seth Godin says in *Meatball Sundae,* it's no good just bunging 'some of that Internet stuff' (the sundae) on top of a conventional business (the meatballs) and hoping to get somewhere. The result will be a mess. *Creative Disruption* (2010) explains what you need to do to shake up your business in a digital world. We are in the middle of an era of creative disruption. It started with the launch of the first web browser in 1993 and will continue for at least another decade. The term is a hybrid of Joseph Schumpeter's notion of creative destruction and Clayton Christensen's disruptive innovation.

This disruption is caused by new businesses either providing something completely new or something traditional but in a radically improved way. Incumbent businesses are thus faced with a stark choice of reinvention or oblivion (his language, not mine – oblivion sounds rather dramatic). The Internet has created a new physics of business, whereby the rules of who can compete in which market have been completely rewritten. Four forces are at work, he says: entrepreneurs and new entrants, consumers' needs and desires, the proliferation of connected devices, and economic volatility. These forces don't sound particularly new, but Waldman claims that if businesses are to weather this, they need to:

1. Transform the core

Stick to what you do but reinvent how you do it.

2. Find big adjacencies
Use your capabilities to find new business areas.

3. Innovate at the edges
It is here that you will find ways to transform or find adjacencies.

Warren Buffet coined the term *economic moat* to describe the ability a company has to maintain competitive advantage over its rivals. The Internet saw a lot of these economic moats filled in, especially with the removal of geographical boundaries, new distribution methods and the disappearance of intermediaries in many markets. Strategy is not about avoiding unforeseen circumstances – it's about making sure you can deal with them when they do arise (we saw this in Chapter 1 with Philip Kotler's *Chaotics Management System*). Companies need the right people to deal with all of this, and that means getting a blend of fire starters (to spark action), rock stars (that people will follow) and fixers (to make things happen).

The one-sentence summary
**To survive in a digital world, companies need
to transform the core, find big adjacencies,
and innovate at the edges.**

He also believes it is crucial to set up businesses that will cannibalise your existing business, if only because someone else will do it if you don't. He could find no examples of businesses that successfully dealt with competitive pressure without an element of 'the C word'. It is not what companies would ordinarily choose to do, but in many ways the fear of it is as dangerous as cannibalisation itself. Businesses who have adapted successfully did five main things:

1. **They started early**

2. **Their Internet businesses have always been free to compete with their traditional businesses**

3. **They were forced to think internationally**

4. **They continually repeat and refine their processes**

5. **The core still counts**

This is a book that brings invaluable clarity to the turbulent effects of the Internet so far. The author doesn't claim to know where he's taking us next, but rightly warns of the dramatic change ahead. This balance is true of many such books. There are many that chronicle what the Internet has done to businesses, and very few that predict what will happen next. Admittedly, this may be because it is an impossible brief.

People do some very strange things

MICROTRENDS, MARK J. PENN
Subtitled *Surprising tales of the way we live our lives today,* this book looks at 75 groups who, by virtue of their daily decisions, are forging the shape of America and the world. *Microtrends* (2008) is a different take on the big stuff – the macro trends that usually get everyone excited. What these smaller groups have in common is that they are relatively unseen, either because their actual numbers are small or because conventional wisdom hides their potential in the

shadows, sometimes even emphasising the exact opposite of what they are really doing. There are too many to mention them all, but among the groups he identifies are:

1. **Extreme commuters**
   Plenty of couples commute hundreds of miles every day or week as part of a 'normal' life.

2. **Internet marrieds**
   A huge number of happily married couples met online.

3. **Ardent amazons**
   Taller women can handle some physical jobs just as easily as men.

4. **Southpaws unbound**
   There are an increasing number of left-handers now that it is no longer such a taboo.

5. **Late-breaking gays**
   Plenty of men marry women first and then change their minds.

6. **Mildly disordered teens**
   A huge percentage of US teenagers are on medication, often suggested by their parents.

7. **Vegan children**
   More and more children are specifying highly demanding dietary requirements.

8. **Shy millionaires**
   There is a significant minority who have no splashy lifestyle but amass a lot of cash, and certainly more than a million.

9. **Uptown tattooed**

   The huge increase in people having tattoos is mainly fuelled by the wealthy.

10. **Video game grown-ups**

   Many of those who started playing when they were younger never stopped.

This is a motley crew of people doing strange things, or representing enough of a small movement to call it a trend. The knack for marketers is to discover such microtrends early enough to do something about them, since many of the groups represent an increasing business opportunity. This is particularly the case if no one else has cottoned on to their needs or done anything to meet them.

The one-sentence summary
There may be a microtrend developing that represents an opportunity.

The book is full of chances for marketers to find a new audience, but it is also a chance for the rest of us to learn something that would make good dinner table conversation. Without wishing to decry the accuracy of the information in the book, here we enter the amusing world of *factoids*. The word was coined by the US author Norman Mailer, and is defined as 'a piece of unreliable information believed to be true because of the way it is presented or repeated in print'. Strange factoids in *Microtrends* include:

1. **There are more Christian Zionists than Jewish ones**

2. **One per cent of young Californians want to grow up to be military snipers**

3. **As a result of the crime crackdown, one of the fastest-growing population segments is newly released ex-convicts**

4. **Knitting is experiencing a revival among young people**

5. **Those who love technology are more outgoing than those who hate technology**

In a way, these discoveries leave us everywhere and nowhere. The information probably only has highly precise application if the group in question has direct relevance to you or your business. The book does not offer much analysis of particular products or positions that such groups might like, but in the brief concluding section there is an effort to pull it all together. In a world with more choices, people will fragment in their selections, it concludes (Chris Anderson's *The Long Tail* already told us this). Perhaps more helpfully, it would be a good discipline if marketers checked regularly to see if there are any microtrends developing in areas directly relevant to them.

Social media has changed everything

SOCIALNOMICS, ERIK QUALMAN
Social media is transforming the way we live and do business. This is a massive socio-economic shift that is fundamentally changing the way consumers and companies communicate with each other. According to Erik Qualman, traditional marketing strategies are obsolete, and have been replaced by *Socialnomics* (2009), where online communities influence companies and markets. Brands can now be

strengthened or destroyed by social media. Advertising is less effective. Companies and customers can now connect direct. Word of mouth is now World of mouth – international instantly. Social media provides a preventative role: what happens in Vegas now stays on YouTube, so you need to be careful if you misbehave, but it also provides a steadying influence. On the downside, it facilitates *braggadocian behaviour* – a self-centred approach in which 'it's all about me'. Another drawback is an erosion of confidence in meeting and communicating with people in person. As the author notes, 'the next generation can't speak'.

The old adage that you can only have two out of three of cheap, quick or quality isn't true in social media – you can have all three because someone may already have done part of it for you. It also increases efficiency by eliminating multiple individual redundancies. He defines *Socialommerce,* in which billions of dollars will be made in and around social media. On a personal level, people don't care what Google thinks, they care what their peers and neighbours think.

The one-sentence summary
**Social media is transforming the way we live
and do business.**

Schizophrenic behaviour, in which individuals and companies have different work and play personalities, will disappear as they become the same thing. Companies need to be aware of this too – they can't be one thing and pretend they are something else to their customers. A couple of specific examples of how social media can really change things, from each end of the age spectrum:

1. **Apple have hired a 22-year-old who has never sent an email**
   He has always used instant message, text, phone or social media.

2. **An 83-year-old prints out his social media updates to find out what is contributing to a full life**
   On discovering any 'unfruitful activities', he ceases them immediately.

The first point shows how our reliance on company email in recent times could soon become obsolete. The second shows how older generations are perfectly capable of adopting so-called young technologies, and can even go so far as to use them in a highly clinical way. Keeping an eye on trends and moods has always been both complex and simple. Companies and individuals often struggle to do it well, because things go up and down all the time. The knack is to stay interested and informed so that you can act early enough to take advantage of what's happening.

CHAPTER 4 WISDOM

- We need to learn constantly to keep adapting to an ever-changing world.

- The rules of the physical world do not apply online: everything is now miscellaneous.

- Numbers can ruin lives. They are repeatedly misused and misunderstood, so make sure you understand your data properly.

- Ignore important-sounding but resonance-free offerings and concentrate on bridging the gap between what you deliver and what consumers want.

- To survive in a digital world, companies need to transform the core, find big adjacencies, and innovate at the edges.

- There may be a microtrend developing that represents an opportunity.

- Social media is transforming the way we live and do business.

CHAPTER 5. CREATIVITY: HOW CAN WE INSPIRE IT, AND CAN ANYONE DO IT?

There's a lot of brainpower around

COGNITIVE SURPLUS, CLAY SHIRKY

Everywhere you go, businesses are preoccupied with crea-tivity. Gone are the days when companies just made stuff and sold it to a deliriously grateful customer base. Now it's all about the big idea – not that anyone has ever specified how you judge the difference between a big one and a small one. But the race is on, and that means severe pressure for employees in companies that are striving for this elusive creativity. How does an executive suddenly become 'crea-tive', if it's not their natural thing?

Don't panic, says Clay Shirky in *Cognitive Surplus* (2010). In the post-industrial world, there has been a huge increase in the number of people paid to think and talk, rather than to produce or transport objects, and they are getting pretty good at it. We now have free time on a scale like never before, but for most of the second half of the last century, most people just used it to sit and watch television. TV viewing is now in decline for the first time, and the world is beginning to use the cognitive surplus generated by this free time to become involved in active participation rather than passive consumption.

Subtitled *Creativity and generosity in a connected age,* the book uses a mixture of example, analysis and social theory to suggest why a new generation is making choices that contribute to a greater whole. We now have the means, motive and opportunity to experiment with ideas at almost no cost, and amongst a huge base of potential users. Tapping this surplus benefits everybody. The cognitive surplus, newly forged from previously disconnected islands of time and talent, is just raw material. To get any value out of it, we have to make it mean or do things.

Old logic is television logic. TV audiences didn't create any real value for each other. In fact, TV raises material aspirations and anxiety, but the only way to do anything about it is to buy goods. Instead, we need to rethink our concept of media – it's not something we consume, it's something we use. By contrast, he says, the Internet succumbs to post-Gutenberg economics. No one in particular owns it, and everyone can use it. There are three types of group production:

1. **Private sector**

   A group does something for less than its selling price.

2. **Public sector**

   Obliged to work together on something of perceived high value.

3. **Social**

   This is value creation without price signals and managerial oversight.

The one-sentence summary
More and more people are using their free time to become involved in active participation.

People are 'hopelessly committed' both to being individual and collective. In chemistry, bonding atoms have valence. In social production, contributors need a 'positive normative or ethical valence toward the process'. In other words, people love getting involved, and they aren't usually in it for financial reasons. They just need to be motivated in the right way. Shirky has some suggestions for harnessing the cognitive surplus that might be useful to provide the impetus for ideas:

1. **Starting**
   Start small; ask why?; behaviour follows opportunity; default to social.

2. **Growing**
   One hundred users are harder than 12 and 1,000; people differ, more people differ more; intimacy doesn't scale; support a supportive culture.

3. **Adapting**
   The faster you learn, the sooner you'll be able to adapt; success causes more problems than failure; clarity is violence; try anything, try everything.

Somewhere in this curious voluntary arena is where trends emerge and opinions form. It's not a science, but it is an important area that marketers need to be familiar with, even though they cannot control it in conventional ways. It's more about catching the spirit of a thought generated by a relevant group, or seeding an idea and watching it take on a life of its own.

You never know what's there until you have a look

POKE THE BOX, SETH GODIN
Our old friend Seth Godin is usually causing a stir of one kind or another, and as we saw in Chapter 4, in 2011 he did a deal with Amazon to publish e-books, which he called The Domino Project.

Perhaps not surprisingly, the first e-book he published was one of his own. Called *Poke the Box* and subtitled *When was the last time you did something for the first time?*, it is a manifesto about starting things, making a ruckus and taking what feels like a risk. The origin of the title comes from his experience as a child: a buzzer box has some lights and switches on it – when you poke it, things happen. In our adult lives, he exhorts us to adopt the same inquisitive approach. When I do this, what happens?; What can you start?; Soon is not as good as now. When the cost of poking the box is less than the cost of doing nothing, then you should poke. Poking isn't about being right. It means action. He outlines seven imperatives:

1. **Be aware**
   ...of the market, opportunities, and who you are.

2. **Be educated**
   ...so you can understand what is around you.

3. **Be connected**
   ...so you can be trusted as you engage.

4. **Be consistent**
   ...so the system knows what to expect.

5. **Build an asset**
   ...so you have something to sell.

6. **Be productive**
   ...so you can be well-priced.

7. **Have the guts and heart and passion to ship**
   Get whatever you have produced out of the door.

As ever with a list of instructions, some are easier said than done, and the imperatives need scrutiny. Yes, we should be aware of what's going on. To a degree we can 'be educated' – we can thirst for knowledge, within the limitations of our mental capability. Being connected takes a lot of time and effort, and crucially it requires a delicate balance between giving and taking in the online world. Being productive, building an asset and shipping some product is far more challenging – arguably not everyone is cut out for that (we saw Steven Pressman's take on shipping in Chapter 3).

The one-sentence summary
Pick yourself to be inquisitive and create something.

Human nature is to need a map. Stop waiting for one, Godin says. If you're brave enough to draw one, people will follow. The challenge is getting into the habit of starting. Anxiety is experiencing failure in advance. If you are anxious about starting a project, then you will associate risk with failure. Starting means you're going to finish. The whole book is a call to arms. What could you build? Followers want to be picked for promotion, praise or some other credit. They are saying: 'Pick me!'. You should reject the tyranny of 'picked' and pick yourself. Excellence isn't about working extra hard to do what you're told; it's about taking the initiative to do work you decide is worth doing.

'This might not work' is a healthy approach. Focus on the work, not the fear that comes from doing the work. The person who fails the most usually wins. Juggling is about throwing, not catching. If you get better at throwing, the catches take care of themselves. The Dandelion Mind idea is engaging: dandelions produce 2,000 seeds a year and it doesn't matter where they land. Produce a lot and things will happen.

Oblique approaches work better than direct ones

OBLIQUITY, JOHN KAY

Creative thinking doesn't work very well when you try to stampede from A to B to generate a result. Paradoxically, many goals are more likely to be achieved when pursued indirectly, so says John Kay in *Obliquity* (2010). The most profitable companies are not the most aggressive in chasing profits, the wealthiest people are not the most materialistic, and the happiest people do not pursue happiness as a specific goal in its own right. This is the concept of 'obliquity'. (The profit-seeking paradox echoes Collins & Porras in *Built to Last* – the most successful companies did not put profit first).

Oblique approaches often take a step back to move forward. Apparently daunting tasks are made easier by doing *something,* and then learning. This approach is often more fruitful than laboriously detailed planning. Charles Lindblom described it as *The Science of Muddling Through.* On top of this, direct approaches are often impracticable because the world is too complex, so problem-solving needs to be iterative and adaptive. Kay highlights the differences between direct and oblique approaches. I have stated the oblique approach first for clarity:

1. **Loosely defined and multi-dimensional objectives**
   v. Objectives that are clear, and can be defined and quantified.

2. **No clear distinction between goals and actions**
   v. A clear distinction between goals and actions, and how to achieve them.

3. **Actions and context influence next action**
   v. Interactions with others are limited.

4. **Imperfect knowledge, learnt on the way**
   v. Structure of relationships clearly understood.

5. **Only a limited number of options identified or perceived as available**
   v. Range of options, fixed and known.

6. **Outcomes arise through complex processes no one fully grasps**
   v. What happens is what we intend to happen.

7. **Recognise that only limited knowledge is available**
   v. Decisions made on the basis of the fullest possible information.

8. **Good outcomes derived through continual, often unsuccessful, adaptation**
   v. Best outcomes through a conscious process of maximisation.

This is the sort of list that strikes fear in the hearts of controlling companies and marketers the world over. Surely it is better to follow a well-defined process and control every step of it? Kay says no. Better results are achieved by letting go and deciding what to do next once the current thing has been done and observed.

The one-sentence summary
Our goals are best achieved indirectly, so consider taking the oblique route.

Judgements about feelings, rather than the feelings themselves, explain why we do things that involve hardship, such as parenthood or mountaineering, he maintains. Being creative, or even just trying to achieve something, often works much better when we adopt the indirect approach. Eudaimonia (often spelt eudemonia) is a high-level concept – a measure of quality of life, of fulfilling one's potential, and making sense of seemingly contradictory actions. Originally invented by Aristotle, it means happiness resulting from a rational active life.

One of his most brilliantly subversive points is that decision-making models are not used to inform decision-making, but to justify decisions that have already been made. Business executives (and marketers?) are past masters at this, but it is illusory. Compare the world to a game of Sudoku. There is only one solution; we know when we have found it; play is not influenced by the responses of others; there is a complete list of possible actions; and complexity has a limit. But human brains work on real problems, not artificial ones, and in that context, none of those rules apply. That is why, in an imperfect world, obliquity works best.

You can do business and have fun

THE BUSINESS PLAYGROUND, STEWART & SIMMONS

There are many who take business very seriously, and the way some executives carry on in meetings you would be forgiven for thinking that it truly is a matter of life and death. But grown-ups can rediscover the magic of creativity that we all had as children, and apply it to business, according to Dave Stewart and Mark Simmons in *The Business Playground* (2010). The problem is that most people 'unlearn' how to do it. If the name Dave Stewart rings a bell, you'd be right. Having the Eurythmics man as a co-author is appealing, but in truth he just adds an anecdote at the end of each chapter.

Creative brilliance is possible when we allow ourselves to move outside the expected, whereas education and work stifle our natural creative talents, the authors argue. There are lots of ways of doing this, and here are a few of their suggestions:

1. Idea spaghetti

Having lots of ideas increases the likelihood that some will be good – 'idea spaghetti'. This is of course the opposite of honing down too early to arrive at just the one winner.

2. Not accepting the status quo

This is a good starting point for innovation. It's important to be constantly curious and looking for things to improve. What bugs you most about something? Now work out how to improve it.

3. **Asking the right questions**

   This increases the chances of finding the right solutions – 'the answer is in the question'. Assumptions need to be scrutinised.

4. **Taking your mind off solving a problem**

   ...increases your chance of solving it.

5. **Visualising ideas**

   ...helps free up creative thinking, but evocative language also helps. So does taking time with the details so they are as vivid as possible.

6. **Thinking big helps**

   ...as does trying on other people's shoes, and using orchestrated chaos. Others will certainly see things differently to you.

7. **Murdering bad ideas**

   Kill those that aren't worth spending time on, and then choose the big one and put it into orbit.

The one-sentence summary
Unlearn your serious side and relearn how creativity can stimulate commerce.

There are lots of techniques and games to help train your creative muscles. The authors' view is that creativity and commerce can collide to great effect if we allow ourselves to free up proper play-based thinking. Many companies are slaves to *convergent thinking* that converges on one single answer, whereas *divergent thinking* has many possible answers. This is much more likely to be fruitful because it has a greater propensity to generate the unexpected.

Interestingly, the brain prepares itself to come up with an insight even before it has solved a problem, so it's fine to relax into this process and let it happen naturally. As any self-respecting creative professional will tell you, it is important when looking for good ideas to ignore the most obvious creative solutions or at the very least put them to one side. Creativity is about making connections between two seemingly unconnected things. In this respect, unlike the tired mantra from brainstorms that 'there is no such thing as a bad idea', there most certainly is. We therefore need the ability to disregard them without recourse and move on to something better.

The mind needs software too

THINK!, EDWARD DE BONO

Our current way of thinking is not good enough, and here's what we can do about it, claims world-renowned thinker Edward de Bono in *Think!* (2009). While our methods are excellent when applied to science and technology, when we attempt to tackle more human issues like climate change and war, we make no progress at all. And this criticism could equally be levelled at businesses and their approach to thinking creatively. There are various types of important thinking, and he stresses two in particular:

1. Perceptual thinking
This is more powerful than logic in changing behaviour, because perception has more bearing on what is going on than logic.

2. Exploratory thinking

This is more likely to achieve progress than argument because it allows for possibilities rather than reiterating entrenched positions.

Critical thinking, as espoused by the Greek Gang of Three (Socrates, Plato and Aristotle), is excellent but not enough. It is fine for destroying ideas but not for creating new ideas in the first place. He argues that those who claim that the term 'problem-solving' covers everything are effectively suggesting that 'anything you want to do' forms a problem, which includes any mental activity. This is misleading and dangerous because it excludes all other forms of thinking. Not all thinking involves problems, so it doesn't pay to start from a negative position. In business there is an obvious need for new thinking, because you can argue till you are blue in the face that you are right, and still go bankrupt a month later. Companies need to be aware of this and start concentrating on ways to discuss change. A 'proto-truth' describes something we hold to be true, providing we are trying to change it. This can be more creatively fruitful than the belief that we already have the true answer. As the old saying goes, the mark of an intelligent mind is the ability to hold two opposing thoughts at the same time.

The one-sentence summary

Our current way of thinking is not good enough – perceptual and exploratory thinking are more powerful than critical thinking.

As you might expect from someone who has written so much on thinking, he reworks many of his old techniques, so you may have seen some of them before. That is not to dismiss their value. Three in particular have specific merit in relation to creativity:

1. Provocative Operation

He often uses the initials PO before announcing a thought. This signifies the beginning of a new, usually lateral, thought and can also be linked to possible, hypothesis, pose, potential, and so on. Interjected into conversations, PO has the power to push thinking along faster and more productively.

2. Operacy

This is just as important as literacy and numeracy. It's the skill of operating or getting things done, but schools only really concentrate on the first two. As we see so often in business, ideas are only as useful as the ability to enact them.

3. The Septine

This is a new concept in which you write down seven different thoughts about a situation. There is no logical sequence and it is not analysis; they are merely scattered elements that could lead to better thoughts.

At the beginning of the last chapter we looked at Bill Lucas arguing that we need a new kind of *mind-ware* – ways to develop our adaptive intelligence. His *mind-ware* consists of personal habits of mind and patterns of social interaction that he believes need to evolve constantly in order for us to cope with changing times. Similarly, de Bono's techniques are often referred to as software for the mind – better mental approaches that get us out of a cerebral rut and into more clever ways of dealing with the issues that vex us.

Creative exercises can help

STICKY WISDOM, MATT KINGDON ET AL.

Matt Kingdon set up one of the first innovation companies in the United Kingdom called What If? In *Sticky Wisdom,* he and his colleagues outline their philosophy and explain a process, with related workshop exercises, that will allow you to follow their approach. Originally produced in 2002 (and entitled *What If?),* it claims that you can start a creative revolution at work by thinking and behaving differently. The secret lies in simple, practical learning about how creativity works. It is something of a call to arms – encouraging companies to manage the human mind more effectively, to add value and uniqueness to what they do, and to liberate creativity and innovation. You can easily follow the techniques for being more creative. They are:

1. Freshness

The quality of the initial stimulus has a direct bearing on how good the final ideas are. River jumping exercises here include re-expression, looking at related worlds, revolution via challenging assumptions, and making random links.

2. Greenhousing

Young ideas need protection when they are at their most vulnerable. SUN = Suspend judgement + Understand + Nurture – these are helpful qualities. RAIN = React + Assume + Insist – this will kill most ideas immediately.

3. **Realness**

Once you stop talking and start doing you can make real progress. The skill is to bring the idea to life very early rather than keep talking about it, which is why prototypes are a great idea.

4. **Momentum**

You need to dismantle barriers and generate 'unreasonable urgency'. Seek alignment, create crisis, say no to distractions, and channel a lot of energy into the task at hand.

5. **Signalling**

This is an enabling characteristic that strengthens and sustains ideas. It is crucial to navigate between the analytical and creative world. Tune in + Choose to act + Propose a response = a helpful sequence to elicit reaction and arrive somewhere constructive.

6. **Courage**

Overcoming mediocrity and being brave is essential. Show your struggle, stretch your comfort zone, get convicted, and carry that enthusiasm along with the idea.

The one-sentence summary

To hatch a decent creative idea you need to have high-quality stimulus, protect and nurture young ideas, and use unreasonable urgency to move rapidly to a prototype that will evoke a reaction.

This is a book that has plenty of good ideas but is also very much a brochure for the company. That aside, it really helps to grapple with potentially random brainstorm meetings and give them a bit of proper shape with some effective exercises. There are a few good ones here that you can copy. Many of them are similar to those in other books, such as Adam Morgan's *Eating the Big Fish* (re-expression and reframing); *The Brand Innovation Manifesto* by John Grant (related worlds and category stealing); and Wayne Lotherington's *Flicking your Creative Switch* (random links and random words). That's not necessarily a bad thing, since it is probably not a surprise that similar approaches to idea generation in business really can work.

You can try using a system

ZAG, Marty Neumeier

If you can't generate a decent idea with any of the approaches mentioned so far, then there may be no hope for you or your company. If this is because people prefer a clearly defined method, then the one proposed in *Zag* (2007) may be for you. In an age of me-too products and instant communications, it argues, keeping up with the competition is no longer a winning strategy. You have to out-position, out-manoeuvre, and out-design everyone else. When everybody else zigs, you should zag. Radical differentiation is the number one strategy of high-performance brands. There is a 17-step process for working all this out (there is more detail to each but the highlights are here):

1. **Who are you?**
   Where do you have the most credibility and experience?

2. **What do you do?**
   What business are you in? What is your purpose?

3. **What's your vision?**
   What do you want to accomplish in 5, 10, 20 years?
   Paint a vivid picture of your future.

4. **What wave are you riding?**
   Make a list of trends that will power your success.

5. **Who shares the brandscape?**
   Who else competes in the category? How does your
   brand rank with customers?

6. **What makes you the 'only'?**
   What's the one thing that makes you different?
   Complete an 'onliness' statement.

7. **What should you add or subtract?**
   Decide what to keep, sacrifice or add.

8. **Who loves you?**
   Draw a diagram of your brand's ecosystem and decide
   how each participant will contribute and benefit.

9. **Who's the enemy?**
   Tell your customers what you're not, in no uncertain
   terms.

10. **What do they call you?**
    Choose a name that is different, brief and appropriate.

11. **How do you explain yourself?**
    What's the one true statement you can make about
    your brand? Craft a 'trueline' that makes it compelling.

12. How do you spread the word?
Align all your communications with your zag, and make sure they are as different as your brand.

13. How do people engage with you?
See which areas you can avoid entirely, and those where you'll be unopposed.

14. What do they experience?
Map the customer journey from non-awareness to full enrolment.

15. How do you earn their loyalty?
Start by being loyal to customers, give them the tools to introduce new ones, and don't make new ones feel punished or excluded.

16. How do you extend your success?
Choose between a house of brands and a branded house. Only add extensions that reinforce the brand's meaning.

17. How do you protect your portfolio?
Avoid C-Sickness – contagion, confusion, contradiction and complexity.

The one-sentence summary
When everybody else zigs, you should zag. Radical differentiation is the number one strategy of high-performance brands.

That's quite a lot to take in at one go, and of course these techniques are at their most effective when you work through them step by step. Although it may look as though there's a lot involved, in fact this is a short, inspirational book and you can follow the sequence and apply it to a brand pretty swiftly. Each step also has a set of subsidiary questions that allows you to investigate deeper on an issue if you want. We have seen most of these questions before, of course, but it is inventively packaged so it sustains interest. So there are many ways to stimulate creativity. Being inquisitive, heading off at angles, having fun with it, using exercises and realising that the mind needs software too, can all play their part.

CHAPTER 5 WISDOM

- **More and more people are using their free time to become involved in active participation.**

- **Pick yourself to be inquisitive and create something.**

- **Our goals are best achieved indirectly, so consider taking the oblique route.**

- **Unlearn your serious side and relearn how creativity can stimulate commerce.**

- **Our current way of thinking is not good enough – perceptual and exploratory thinking are more powerful than critical thinking.**

- **To hatch a decent creative idea you need to have high quality stimulus, protect and nurture young ideas and use unreasonable urgency to move rapidly to a prototype that will evoke a reaction.**

- **When everybody else zigs, you should zag. Radical differentiation is the number one strategy of high-performance brands.**

CHAPTER 6.
OBSERVATION AND LANGUAGE: IT'S ALL IN THE TELLING

Why do we speak like this?

THE LANGUAGE WARS, HENRY HITCHINGS

Marketing involves communication. And communication requires language. It could be visual language, but a large part of it is verbal. We communicate all day, whether that is a company trying to get across a certain feature or benefit to a customer, or colleagues discussing the pros and cons of their approaches. It's all in the telling. And yet so much of the language we use is redundant, nonsensical and poorly considered. Marketing in particular is notorious for the way it embraces bullshit and cliché. So it seems reasonable that a thorough analysis of how we observe things and deploy language could help us to be better understood in both a corporate and personal context.

The Language Wars (2011) unpacks how the history of 'proper' English came about. It looks at grammar rules, regional accents, swearing, spelling, dictionaries, political correctness and the role of electronic media in reshaping language. People get angry about English, as you can immediately see from the letters page on many a national newspaper. They argue about slang, abbreviations, buzzwords (itself a buzzword?), vocabulary imported from other languages, the abuse of apostrophes, and the mistakes of public figures who they believe 'ought to know better'.

But people have always worried about the state of the English language, from Chaucer through to Dickens and Shakespeare to the modern day. Rules are a sort of armour, and yet rule-makers miss out on the dynamism of speech. Rules are really mental mechanisms that carry out operations to combine words in helpful arrangements so we can be understood. The author is not arguing that there should be no norms or rules – just that we ought to think beyond tradition, habit and deference, and to consider what we want from our words. We need to engage with language more effectively. We tend to discuss it in a cantankerous or petulant way, but thinking and talking about it should be a pleasure.

The one-sentence summary

We need to engage with language more – thinking and talking about it in a more effective way.

This is a series of 28 pithy essays that guide us through the history of our language, from slang and spelling to text messaging. Given the recent rise of English as the world's default Internet language, it is particularly important that we look at it carefully and understand it. We all have our pet hates, but these start to look rather foolish if you take the long view. Jonathan Swift hated the words 'mob' and 'banter'. Dr Johnson hated 'trait' and 'ruse', mainly because they were French in origin. Not long ago 'mileage' and 'hindsight' were regarded as awful Americanisms. Things move on. Complaints about English are as old as the hills, based on no particular linguistic logic. It is also a fairly futile pursuit, since no one can stop language from evolving, and it is healthy that it does.

The reader can either regard this book as a call to arms, or just a pleasant ramble through the vagaries of our strange language. The main message is to take the long view and not get too agitated by the details. Far more important is our ability to communicate clearly as individuals and companies.

Even academics have a view

ON BULLSHIT, HARRY G. FRANKFURT

We all know that the man in the pub can spin a yarn or two, and that a huge proportion of business meetings are full of impenetrable twaddle. What you might not be aware of is that bullshit is equally a subject for discussion in the academic world. Harry G. Frankfurt is a professor at Princeton University and a renowned moral philosopher. His short book *On Bullshit* (2005) is a thoughtful debate on an unusual subject for academia. Witness observations like this one:

'The realms of advertising and of public relations, and the nowadays closely related realm of politics, are replete with instances of bullshit so unmitigated that they can serve among the most indisputable and classic paradigms of the concept.'

Frankfurt observes that bullshit is now ubiquitous but strangely has not attracted much sustained inquiry because we think we know how to spot it and deal with it. Nor is it easy to define because the term is often used loosely and as a generic term of abuse – it covers a multitude of sins. We talk so much of this stuff that we have a multitude of words for it. Synonyms for humbug (suggested by Max Black in 1985) include balderdash, buncombe, claptrap, drivel, hokum, imposture, quackery and many more.

Constituent elements of bullshit are deceptive misrepresentation, just short of lying, especially by pretentious word or deed, and distortion of somebody's own thoughts, feelings or attitudes. Frankfurt deconstructs these elements and compares bullshit to shoddy goods – produced in a careless or self-indulgent manner, and never finely crafted. The essence of bullshit is a lack of concern with the truth and an indifference to how things really are. It involves a kind of bluff.

Does the bullshitter lie? Not necessarily. He or she is phony rather than false. The bullshitter is faking things, but this does not mean that he or she necessarily gets them wrong. As such, bullshitters have much more freedom than someone who tells the truth or lies, because they do not require an anchor point on one side or the other. The production of bullshit is stimulated whenever a person's obligations or opportunities to speak about something exceed their knowledge of the facts that are relevant to the topic.

The one-sentence summary
Bullshit is harder to spot than you think because it is neither on the side of the truth nor the false.

As you might expect from an academic, it is a well-researched argument containing a series of very quotable home truths:

'The truth-values of (the bullshitter's) statements are of no central interest to him; what we are not to understand is that his intention is neither to report the truth nor to conceal it.'

'He is neither on the side of the truth nor on the side of the false.'

'He does not care whether the things he says describe reality correctly. He just picks them out, or makes them up, to suit his purpose.'

'He does not reject the authority of truth, as the liar does, and oppose himself to it. He pays no attention to it at all.'

This is an academic essay, not a 'pop' book, so you need to concentrate on the line of argument carefully, but you can read it in an hour, which helps. At the very least it signals that bullshit needs to be taken seriously. Should you be genuinely duped by it, things could get awkward. It's more insidious than you might think, so it pays to be on the lookout for it so that you can react appropriately and not act on falsehoods.

Be careful what you say

EXCEPTIONAL SERVICE, EXCEPTIONAL PROFIT,
INGHILLERI & SOLOMON

Having difficulty with language in the meeting room is one thing, but it takes on a completely different complexion when companies are dealing with customers. This is vitally important in any service industry. Delivering brilliant service leads to higher profits via customer loyalty. But getting it wrong can lead to all sorts of problems, say Inghilleri & Solomon in *Exceptional Service, Exceptional Profit*, (2010). The irony is that the process only needs to be mastered once and then the rules can be applied successfully for a lifetime. There are five important elements to it:

1. **Selecting, training and inspiring loyalty virtuosos at all levels**

2. **Handling service breakdowns in a systematic way that makes customers more loyal than if the mishap hadn't happened**

3. **Gathering and using customer preference data**

4. **Ensuring you meet customers' timeliness and quality expectations**

5. **Personalising the experience of online customers**

All of this involves the careful use of language to communicate and understand. The four main elements of customer satisfaction are perfect product, caring delivery, timeliness, and an effective problem-resolution process. In a service business, you can't achieve this without the right language. So language engineering is vitally important. A consistent style of speech comes from an established lexicon of preferred language and phrasing that everyone should be trained to use.

The one-sentence summary

Train your people to speak in the right way with their colleagues and customers.

If you work in a service industry you can take the examples from the book and apply them. For example, the four steps to great service recovery with customers are:

1. **Apologise**

2. **Review the complaint with the customer**

3. **Fix the problem and follow up**

4. **Document it to stop it happening again**

If the context involves a colleague, this sequence could equally read: acknowledge it, review it, fix it, write it down, and stop it happening again. Keeping track of customer preferences is an almost guaranteed way to keep them coming back. You need a simple system that can be accessed in real time, but beware making assumptions because of course their preferences can change. With regard to your colleagues, you can work through an organisation from the leaders to the most junior staff to inculcate them with a service ethic, which affects recruitment, training and reinforcement. If you tell them what language is and isn't expected, they can learn fast, and keep a closer watch on how they express what they are trying to say.

We do talk a lot of rubbish

WHY BUSINESS PEOPLE SPEAK LIKE IDIOTS, FUGERE ET AL. So much for a serious take on the importance of business language. In 2005 Fugere, Hardaway & Warshawsky put the issue of bullshit firmly under the microscope in *Why Business People Speak Like Idiots*. Bull has become the official language of business, they say, and it's out of control. Every day we are bombarded by an endless stream of filtered, antiseptic, jargon-filled corporate speak, all of which makes it harder to get heard, be authentic, and have fun.

The thing is, it doesn't have to be that way, which is why they offer a guide for those who want to get on in business without leaving their personality at the door. The second people get to work they usually trade the wit and warmth of their normal voices for a corporate stamp of approval and the comfort of conformity. This is not because of some evil corporate conspiracy. It's the result of four traps:

1. **The Obscurity Trap**

   Jargon, wordiness and evasiveness are great evils. They can be overcome by avoiding long and pointless words, keeping everything short, and coming to the point.

2. **The Anonymity Trap**

   Corporate clones sound like everyone else. This trap can be overcome by ditching templates, keeping imperfection in presentations to show humanity, using humour, and by picking up the phone.

3. **The Hard-sell Trap**

   Fear, habit and bad role models are all to blame. This can be overcome by using the 'non-sell sell', by kicking the habit of the relentlessly happy messenger, and by apologising properly for mistakes.

4. **The Tedium Trap**

   Most people ignore things (*'And this is interesting because?'*). You can overcome this by entertaining people, bringing things to life, using their point to make yours, telling stories, and having style.

The one-sentence summary

Capture people's imagination by avoiding jargon, sameness, hard sell, and boring material.

Although the language the authors use is akin to a pub rant, there are serious messages lurking within. We all have a responsibility to cut out obscure jargon and make ourselves more distinctive. If something seems boring, then admit it and come up with something more interesting. You can rattle through this book fast, laugh at the absurdity of much work language, and pick up some helpful tips for railing against the conformity of work. If you can rise above the traps they specify, it is possible to capture people's imagination, stir their enthusiasm, and tell them the truth. Even at work.

Work out what not to say

BAD LANGUAGE, GRAHAM EDMONDS

Avoidance is an important part of dealing with language at work, says Graham Edmonds in *Bad Language* (2008). Language in the workplace matters because it can inspire or deflate. An essential aspect of any organisation is the way in which it communicates, internally or externally, and the language used can contribute greatly to its potential success, or failure. This is a compendium of words and phrases to avoid in business, that works its way through the departments and considers the chaotic words commonly used by particular culprits such as HR, finance, IT, and of course, marketing.

It is similar to a business bullshit dictionary, but is divided into sections with different types of such language. It tries to deconstruct the worst offending items so that the more thoughtful person at work can avoid them. Garbled words and manipulated phrases are especially dangerous because they can lead to plain deceit, so we all need to be on the lookout for them. Most importantly, the language used can drastically alter the way something is interpreted, so you have a strong chance either of being misunderstood or failing to understand. This can also vary by audience, so great care is needed. Danger areas to look out for in corporate speak include:

1. **Cliché**

   Back to basics, core/non-core, customer-focused, re-engineer, and so on.

2. **Strategy waffle**

   Direction, approach, fit, high/low risk, exit, goals, and more...

3. **Attempted perception change**

   Barriers, benchmarking, best practice, big picture, comfort zone, competitive advantage, continuous improvement...

4. **Euphemism**

   The liar's best friend – disguising something bad in different language, such as getting rid of a member of staff: axed, busted, chopped, cut, fired, terminated, canned, ditched, let go, etc.

5. **Metaphor**

   These are endless: ball juggling, back on the coal face, all singing all dancing, finger on the pulse, cycling with no saddle...

6. **Idiom**

   Bang for your buck, eating your own dog food, riding the razor blade, smoke and mirrors job...

7. **Simile**

   Drive that message home, like herding cats, not comparing apples with apples, having a flight path, as easy as ABC...

8. **Acronyms**
   AFLO (Another F*cking Learning Opportunity),
   ASTRO (Always Stating The Really Obvious), BOHICA
   (Bend Over, Here it Comes Again), PICNIC (Problem In
   Chair Not In Computer)...

The one-sentence summary
**Language in the workplace matters – it can
inspire or deflate, so choose your words
carefully.**

Those working in large organisations need to balance their
annoyance at this type of language with a means of working
with it, because it won't go away, and the constant protestor
could come across as a cynic. Simply railing against the
daftness of it all may not be the best approach if it merely
conveys that you can see how ridiculous the language is.
Far better that someone develops a reputation for spotting
it and then does something about it. Being a thoughtful pur-
veyor of intelligent language is what decent marketers
should aspire to, both in their own spoken and written
words, and in those of the brands they are marketing.

There is always more than one point of view

WHAT THE DOG SAW, MALCOLM GLADWELL
And finally, you could argue that all this talk about language use is marginal if everybody has a different view
anyway. You'll discover soon enough if no one is agreeing
with you.

Master storyteller Malcolm Gladwell produced *What the
Dog Saw* in 2009. This is not a book on one theme – it is a

compendium of his best essays for the *New Yorker* magazine over the last 10 years or so, organised into three sections: *Obsessives, pioneers, and other varieties of minor genius; Theories, predictions and diagnoses; Personality, character and intelligence.* So it covers a wide palate of human experience, in which observation and language are critical.

The title refers to his take on how Cesar Millan, also known as the Dog Whisperer, does what he does. Gladwell is more interested in the dog's perspective, and it transpires that the dog's response is mainly down to Millan's body language. He teases out scores of curiosities, but here I have drawn out my top 10 favourites:

1. **Most things are not interesting**
   Too many people concentrate on the stuff that isn't.

2. **Perfection is plural**
   Everybody has a different version of it.

3. **Progress often comes in advance of understanding**
   As with the contraceptive pill, the invention exists, but the consequences are not yet clear.

4. **A puzzle is not the same as a mystery**
   Osama bin Laden's whereabouts (at the time of writing) were a puzzle. How Enron collapsed is actually a mystery.

5. **Solving issues means connecting the dots**
   Spotting the sequence is a skill. Many people just can't do it. They simply see ink blots like the Rorschach Test (he was the twentieth-century Swiss psychiatrist who invented it).

6. Creeping determinism is misleading

Claiming retrospectively that something was coherent or made sense all along is a case in point (x apparently determined y, but it didn't really). This affects many business case histories, and much journalism.

7. Choking is loss of instinct

A tennis player reverts to thinking about each shot and loses the game. Panic is reversion to instinct (a diver grabs instinctively for a companion's air supply without realising they can share and both be fine).

8. Risk homeostasis is dangerous

This is where changes intended to make a system safer actually make it worse. When ABS brakes are fitted to cars people drive faster and have more accidents, because they think they are safer.

9. There is no such thing as inherent genius

There are as many late bloomers as there are child prodigies.

10. If everyone has to think outside the box, maybe the box needs fixing

Brilliantly put.

The one-sentence summary

Concentrate on astute observation and clear expression, and remember that there is always another point of view.

One of Gladwell's interviewees suggests that we should stop managing problems and start ending them. Sound words indeed for all of us.

CHAPTER 6 WISDOM

- We need to engage with language more – thinking and talking about it in a more effective way.

- Bullshit is harder to spot than you think because it is neither on the side of the truth nor the false.

- Train your people to speak in the right way with their colleagues and customers.

- Capture people's imagination by avoiding jargon, sameness, hard sell, and boring material.

- Language in the workplace matters – it can inspire or deflate, so choose your words carefully.

- Concentrate on astute observation and clear expression, and remember that there is always another point of view.

APPENDIX I:
A MANIFESTO FOR MARKETERS

40 points that might help your business.

THE BIG ISSUES

- Geographical boundaries have effectively disappeared where business is concerned.
- Turbulence is the new normal – get used to it and develop early-warning systems.
- It's the soft things that matter, and they are very hard to do.
- We live in a complex world of infinite subtleties and variation – don't try to attribute causality when there is none.
- Emotion lies at the heart of consumer behaviour, so it is important to understand exactly how people decide what to buy.
- We are driven by autonomy, mastery and purpose – the desire to direct our own lives, get better at something that matters, and be part of something bigger.

BEHAVIOURAL ECONOMICS

- Economic incentives drive everything.
- Anyone can turn economic reasoning to their own advantage.
- People are predictably irrational when making decisions, and often make basic mistakes.
- The more choice we have, the less we actually make decisions.
- Small changes to the shopping experience can make a huge difference to sales.
- People don't always buy things for the reasons they think they do.
- We have used up most of the breakthroughs that fuelled growth, so stagnation and less choice is the new normal.

ORGANISATIONAL THEORY

- Companies are living entities that thrive by learning, having a strong persona, and governing their growth efficiently.
- Ignore what normal companies do and do the opposite.
- Understanding flocks, schools and colonies can make us better at communicating, decision-making and getting things done.
- A handful of clever star performers create disproportionate amounts of value for organisations, but they must be managed particularly astutely.
- Mapping out a visual canvas of a business model helps you to understand, design, test and implement it more easily than with just words.
- Getting things done involves doggedly overcoming resistance, and having the courage to ship your product.
- You can succeed by paying close attention to how you manage yourself and others.

TRENDS AND MOODS

- We need to unlearn and learn constantly to keep adapting to an ever-changing world.
- The rules of the physical world do not apply online: everything is now miscellaneous.
- Numbers can ruin lives. They are repeatedly misused and misunderstood, so make sure you understand your data properly.
- Ignore important-sounding but resonance-free offerings and concentrate on bridging the gap between what you deliver and what consumers want.
- To survive in a digital world, companies need to transform the core, find big adjacencies, and innovate at the edges.
- There may be a microtrend developing that represents an opportunity.
- Social media is transforming the way we live and do business.

CREATIVITY

- More and more people are using their free time to become involved in active participation.
- Pick yourself to be inquisitive and create something.
- Our goals are best achieved indirectly, so consider taking the oblique route.
- Unlearn your serious side and relearn how creativity can stimulate commerce.
- Our current way of thinking is not good enough – perceptual and exploratory thinking are more powerful than critical thinking.
- To hatch a decent creative idea you need to have high-quality stimulus, protect and nurture young ideas, and use unreasonable urgency to move rapidly to a prototype that will evoke a reaction.
- When everybody else zigs, you should zag. Radical differentiation is the number one strategy of high-performance brands.

OBSERVATION AND LANGUAGE

- We need to engage with language more – thinking and talking about it in a more effective way.
- Bullshit is harder to spot than you think because it is neither on the side of the truth nor the false.
- Train your people to speak in the right way with their colleagues and customers.
- Capture people's imagination by avoiding jargon, sameness, hard sell, and boring material.
- Language in the workplace matters – it can inspire or deflate, so choose your words carefully.
- Concentrate on astute observation and clear expression, and remember that there is always another point of view.

APPENDIX II: THE ONE-MINUTE SUMMARIES

Bad Language GRAHAM EDMONDS

WHAT THE BOOK SAYS
- This is a compendium of words and phrases to avoid in business.
- It is similar to a Business Bullshit dictionary, but is divided into sections with different types of such language, and tries to deconstruct the worst offending items so that the more thoughtful person at work can avoid them.
- Language in the workplace matters because it can inspire or deflate.
- An essential aspect of any organisation is the way in which it communicates, internally or externally, and the language used can contribute greatly to its potential success, or failure.
- Garbled words and manipulated phrases can lead to plain deceit, and we all need to be on the lookout for it.
- The language used can drastically alter the way something is interpreted, and this can also vary by audience, so great care is needed.

WHAT'S GOOD ABOUT IT
- Areas to look out for in corporate speak include:
  - □ cliché: back to basics, core/non-core, customer-focused, re-engineer;
  - □ strategy waffle: direction, approach, fit, high/low risk, exit, goals;
  - □ attempted perception change: barriers, benchmarking, best practice, big picture, comfort zone, competitive advantage, continuous improvement.
- The liar's best friend is the euphemism – disguising something bad in different language, such as getting rid of a member of staff: axed, busted, chopped, cut, fired, terminated, canned, ditched, let go, etc.
- Metaphors are also guilty: ball juggling, back on the coal face, all singing, all dancing, finger on the pulse, cycling with no saddle...
- And so are idioms: bang for your buck, eating your own dog food, riding the razor blade, smoke and mirrors job...

- And the simile: drive that message home, like herding cats, not comparing apples with apples, having a flight path, as easy as ABC...
- And acronyms: AFLO (Another F*cking Learning Opportunity), ASTRO (Always Stating The Really Obvious), BOHICA (Bend Over, Here it Comes Again), PICNIC (Problem In Chair Not In Computer)...

WHAT YOU HAVE TO WATCH
- Not much, but those working in large organisations need to balance their annoyance at this type of language with a means of working with it, because it won't go away, and the constant protestor could come across as a cynic.

Bad Science BEN GOLDACRE

WHAT THE BOOK SAYS
- The author purports to dispense fast and powerful relief from scaremongering journalists, pill-pushing nutritionists, flaky statistics and evil pharmaceutical corporations.
- He dismantles the claims of foolish quacks, via the credence they are given in the mainstream media, and the tricks of the food supplements industry. Scientists and doctors are outnumbered and outgunned by vast armies of individuals who feel entitled to pass judgement on matters of evidence without obtaining a basic understanding of the issues.
- Stories are often the basis of scientific and medical reporting, but the plural of anecdote is not data. Few public examples bear relation to the true issues.
- People are more likely to listen to advice when they have paid for it, so studies verify that the more expensive something is, the more effective it is perceived to be.
- Things can happen at the same time, but that is weak, circumstantial evidence for causation.

WHAT'S GOOD ABOUT IT

- When an honest person speaks, they say only what they believe to be true (liars do the opposite of course). Bullshitters are on neither side. They don't care if they describe reality correctly, so long as they can get away with whatever suits their purpose. The 'opportunity cost' of this is vast.
- Cargo-cult science surrounds itself with all the paraphernalia of science without truly having any. This is based on the cargo cults in the war who saw planes landing with many of the things they desired, and subsequently set up landing strips, wore headphones and antennae made of wood, and waited for more planes. None came.
- PR agencies collude with journalists to generate articles that carry more weight than advertising, or replace it if advertising is not allowed. It also circumnavigates tough restrictions on what can be claimed on packaging, because journalism isn't subject to such rules.
- The real purpose of the scientific method is to make sure nature hasn't misled you into thinking you know something you actually don't know, but clever people believe stupid things when it is presented in a 'sciencey' way.
- Numbers can ruin lives. They are repeatedly misused and misunderstood. This is unfortunate in journalism, but can be fatal in medicine.

WHAT YOU HAVE TO WATCH

- It is not a textbook. You need to use the medical and scientific points and apply them in a business context, because they are analogous.

Business Model Generation OSTERWALDER & PIGNEUR

WHAT THE BOOK SAYS

- This book claims to be a handbook for visionaries, game changers, and challengers striving to defy outmoded business models and design tomorrow's enterprises. No pressure there then.

- It is co-created by 470 strategy practitioners, and provides a rallying call to change the way you think about business models.
- It shows a system moving in a sequence, the main theme of which is the canvas, which has nine building blocks that are constantly reworked throughout:
  □ *Customer segments*
  □ *Value propositions*
  □ *Channels*
  □ *Customer relationships*
  □ *Revenue streams*
  □ *Key resources*
  □ *Key activities*
  □ *Key partnerships*
  □ *Cost structure*
- A variety of patterns is shown, from the Long Tail, to free, open, and multi-sided platforms. The permutations are effectively endless.
- There are then a series of design systems, prototyping and scenario techniques to move from plan to reality, evaluate strategy, design a process, and bring everything to fruition.

WHAT'S GOOD ABOUT IT
- It is presented in a pleasing landscape shape that enables you to view your plans as proper canvases. These are meticulously designed so that you can compare scores of different spreads to view the shape of a business.
- Only the churlish would fail to find a fresh perspective here – you could analyse your business, or a proposed new one, in hundreds of different ways.
- The book is mainly visual, so you don't need to wade through many words to come up with a practical exercise for a planning session.

WHAT YOU HAVE TO WATCH
- The language of business models is always in danger of straying into cliché. Clarity on whether an idea has merit or not should always be screened with a bullshit test.

Buyology MARTIN LINDSTROM

WHAT THE BOOK SAYS
- Subtitled *How Everything We Believe About Why We Buy is Wrong,* the book tries to explain why we don't always buy things for the reasons we think we do. It uses neuromarketing, an intriguing marriage of marketing and science, to provide a window into the human mind.
- Buyology is defined as the subconscious thoughts, feelings and desires that drive purchasing decisions. His main point is that conventional research doesn't work to explain these decisions. Neither quantitative surveys nor qualitative groups correlate well with actual sales. We are a lot better at collecting data than doing anything useful with it.
- His investigations are mildly controversial because they involve hooking respondents up to a range of wires or putting them in scanners. The two main techniques are SST (Steady State Topography) and FMRI (Functional Magnetic Resonance Imaging). They effectively show which parts of the brain react to various stimuli.
- His belief is that by better understanding our seemingly irrational behaviour we can gain more control of our actions.
- Our mirror neurons make us imitate the actions we observe, which is why crazes and marketing phenomena catch on via copying.

WHAT'S GOOD ABOUT IT
- His techniques reveal some interesting things, including:
  - ☐ Product placement doesn't work, even though many companies spend a fortune doing it.

- ☐ Warnings about the perils of smoking can increase smoking because they unintentionally trigger all the (nice) cues that people associate with it.
- ☐ Twelve billion dollars is spent on market research in the United States every year, and yet eight out of 10 new products fail within the first three months, so it doesn't really work.
- ☐ The Pepsi Challenge misled marketers because it was a sip test – drink a whole can and Coke still won.
- ☐ Subliminal messages work, which is why people want to smoke more when in a Marlboro lounge containing imagery subtly reminiscent of the brand.
- ☐ Rituals work, as in the 119.53 seconds it takes to pour a pint of Guinness.
- ☐ Strong brands excite the brain in the same way as religious images.
- ☐ Sex detracts from decent branding. This is the Vampire Effect – sucking attention away from what ads are actually trying to say.

WHAT YOU HAVE TO WATCH
- Not everyone approves of the research techniques because they feel too close to lab experiments.

Chaotics KOTLER & CASLIONE

WHAT THE BOOK SAYS
- Turbulence is now the norm in business, so the *Chaotics Management System* aims to help companies minimise vulnerability and exploit opportunities fast.
- Panic tactics such as staff cuts, price reductions and slashed investment don't work, but early-warning systems do.
- Factors that cause chaos are technological advances and the information revolution, disruptive technologies, the rise of the rest, hypercompetition, sovereign wealth funds, the environment, and customer empowerment.

- The best response is 'skill, will, till': increase spending on new customers, foster a culture to go against the trend, and have some resources to invest.
- Companies need to be responsive, robust and resilient; The most common mistakes made are:
  - ☐ Stretching to attract new customers before you've secured the core
  - ☐ Cutting marketing
  - ☐ Neglecting the 900lb gorilla (everyone knows you're in trouble, so admit it)

WHAT'S GOOD ABOUT IT

- Chaos inflection points can render a strategy obsolete over night.
- There are processes and diagrams that you can map out and enact.
- Business leaders need to see change first hand, eliminate the filers that stop them finding out fast, accept the inevitability of strategy decay, and drop their reliance on a two-playbook strategy – one for up markets and the other for down. The chaotics system has three components:
  - ☐ Detect sources of turbulence through early-warning systems
  - ☐ Respond to chaos by construction of key scenarios
  - ☐ Select strategy based on scenario prioritisation and risk attitude

Anyone can ask the critical questions:

What have been our past blind spots?
Is there an analogy from another industry?
What signals are we rationalising away?
Who is skilled at picking up weak signals and acting on them?
What are our mavericks and outliers trying to tell us?
What future surprises could really hurt or help us?

WHAT YOU HAVE TO WATCH

- It is reasonably serious stuff, so there is no levity to sugar the pill.

Clever GOFFEE & JONES

WHAT THE BOOK SAYS

- You need a particularly astute approach to leading smart, creative people.
- Research shows that a handful of star performers create disproportionate amounts of value for their organisations. They aren't free agents who do this on their own – they need their organisation's commercial and financial resources to fulfil their potential.
- These invaluable individuals are called *clevers* – they can be brilliant, difficult and sometimes even dangerous, and success may well depend on how well they are led, which is a nightmare in itself. Traditional leadership approaches won't be effective. Instead, bosses need to:
  - ☐ *Tell them what the company is doing – but not how to do it*
  - ☐ *Earn their respect with expertise – not a job title*
  - ☐ *Provide 'organised space' for their creativity*
  - ☐ *Sense their needs and keep them motivated*
  - ☐ *Shelter them from administrative and political distractions ('organisational rain')*
  - ☐ *Connect them with clever peers*
  - ☐ *Convince them the company can help them succeed*

WHAT'S GOOD ABOUT IT

- The authors identify *value rationality* – a logic of goals and ends that occur when a company has an aspirational cause. This is an interdependence of equals.
- Getting the approach right works for individuals, teams, and even whole companies – *clevers* attract more *clevers*.
- Their characteristics are: their cleverness is central to their identity; their skills are not easily replicated; they know their worth; they ask difficult questions; they are organisationally savvy; they are not impressed by hierarchy; they expect instant success; they want to be connected to other clever people; they won't thank you.
- Bad characteristics are: they take pleasure in breaking the rules; they trivialise the importance of non-technical

people; they are oversensitive about their projects; they suffer from knowledge-is-power syndrome; they are never happy about the review process.

WHAT YOU HAVE TO WATCH
- Nothing. There is lots here for anyone who has to deal with creative people.

Cognitive Surplus CLAY SHIRKY

WHAT THE BOOK SAYS
- In the post-industrial world, there has been a huge increase in the number of people paid to think and talk, rather than to produce or transport objects.
- We now have free time on a scale like never before, but for most of the second half of the last century, most people just used it to watch TV.
- TV viewing is now in decline for the first time, and the world is beginning to use the cognitive surplus generated by free time to become involved in active participation rather than passive consumption.
- Subtitled *Creativity and generosity in a connected age*, the book uses a mixture of example, analysis and social theory to suggest why a new generation is making choices that contribute to a greater whole.
- We now have the means, motive and opportunity to experiment with ideas at almost no cost, and on a huge base of potential users. Tapping this surplus benefits everybody.

WHAT'S GOOD ABOUT IT
- The cognitive surplus, newly forged from previously disconnected islands of time and talent, is just raw material. To get any value out of it, we have to make it mean or do things.
- Old logic is television logic. TV audiences didn't create any real value for each other. In fact, TV raises material aspirations and anxiety. We need to rethink our concept

of media – it's not something we consume, it's something we use.

- The Internet succumbs to post-Gutenberg economics. No one in particular owns it, and everyone can use it.
- There are three types of group production:
  1. Private sector: a group does something for less than its selling price
  2. Public sector: obliged to work together on something of perceived high value
  3. Social: value creation without price signals and managerial oversight
- People are 'hopelessly committed' both to being individual and collective. In chemistry, bonding atoms have valence. In social production, contributors need a 'positive normative or ethical valence toward the process'.
- Some suggestions for harnessing the cognitive surplus:
  - ☐ Starting: start small; ask why?; behaviour follows opportunity; default to social
  - ☐ Growing: 100 users are harder than 12 and 1,000; people differ, more people differ more; intimacy doesn't scale; support a supportive culture
  - ☐ Adapting: the faster you learn, the sooner you'll be able to adapt; success causes more problems than failure; clarity is violence; try anything, try everything

WHAT YOU HAVE TO WATCH
- It's a great idea but it could have been expressed in an essay rather than a book.

Creative Disruption SIMON WALDMAN

WHAT THE BOOK SAYS
- This is what you need to do to shake up your business in a digital world.
- We are in the middle of an era of creative disruption. It started with the launch of the first web browser in 1993 and will continue for at least another decade. The term is a hybrid of Joseph Schumpeter's notion of creative

destruction and Clayton Christensen's disruptive innovation.

- This disruption is caused by new businesses either providing something completely new or something traditional but in a radically improved way.
- Incumbent businesses are thus faced with a stark choice of reinvention or oblivion.
- The Internet has created a new physics of business, whereby the rules of who can compete in which market have been completely rewritten.
- Four forces are at work: entrepreneurs and new entrants, consumers' needs and desires, the proliferation of connected devices, and economic volatility.
- If businesses are to weather this, they need to:
  1. Transform the core: stick to what you do but reinvent how you do it
  2. Find big adjacencies: use your capabilities to find new business areas
  3. Innovate at the edges: these are either ways to transform or find adjacencies

WHAT'S GOOD ABOUT IT

- Warren Buffet coined the term *economic moat* to describe the ability to maintain competitive advantage over rivals. The Internet saw a lot of these filled in.
- Strategy is not about avoiding unforeseen circumstances – it's about making sure you can deal with them.
- The right people includes a blend of firestarters, rock stars and fixers.
- It is crucial to set up businesses that will cannibalise your business, if only because someone else will do it if you don't.
- A grid covering 'From x, To y' is a good way of organising objectives.
- Businesses who have adapted successfully did five main things:
  1. They started early

2. Their Internet businesses have always been free to
   compete with their traditional businesses
3. They were forced to think internationally
4. They continually repeat and refine their processes
5. The core still counts

WHAT YOU HAVE TO WATCH
- Not much. It is well written, as you would expect from an
  ex-journalist.

Discover Your Inner Economist TYLER COWEN

WHAT THE BOOK SAYS
- Anyone can turn economic reasoning to their advantage
  – at home, work or on holiday.
- Understanding the incentives that work best with each
  individual is the key to satisfactory and successful daily
  interactions, but it only works if we understand the
  importance of respect for human liberty.
- Discovering your inner economist can lead to a happier,
  more satisfying life.
- Good economics should adhere to three tests: *The
  Postcard Test* (write it on the back of one); *The Grandma
  Test* (the theory must be intelligible); and *The Aha
  Principle* (the thought should be a revelation).
- To see patterns in human behaviour, we need to expand
  our repertoire of recognition chunks (chess grandmasters
  can keep 50,000 in their cognitive capacity).
- Psychologists highlight Fundamental Attribution Error or
  correspondence bias: assuming that a single incidence of
  consumer behaviour represents a deep-rooted personality
  trait.
- We make bad decisions when we are under stress.
- In reality we are more typical than we think we are.

WHAT'S GOOD ABOUT IT
- He offers three parables:
  1. *Dirty Dishes* (money doesn't always work: your kids
     will still not do the washing up if you offer to pay)

2. *Car Salesman* (if you don't pay people, they won't do anything)
3. *Parking Tickets* (diplomats from countries with high domestic corruption run up the most parking tickets in New York: people respond to the same incentive in different ways)
- Understanding our approach to culture works best when using two principles of self-management incentives:
  1. *What is scarce? Time, attention or money?*
  2. *We don't care about culture as much as we would like to admit*
- A tragedy of the commons occurs when individual actions, when taken together, destroy the value of an asset or resource. (Is the Mona Lisa over exposed?) In the *Me Factor,* you don't have to pay as much attention to the art as the artist wants you to.
- A third of Londoners buy books 'solely to look intelligent'.
- Selective forgetfulness is the key to many a successful marriage.
- The illusion of group productivity applies to many a group brainstorm.

WHAT YOU HAVE TO WATCH
- It is fairly long and detailed, so you have to dig hard for the nuggets.

Do The Work STEVEN PRESSFIELD

WHAT THE BOOK SAYS
- In short, if you have something to do, then get on with it.
- The great enemies of getting things done are resistance, rational thought, and friends and family.
- Resistance includes fear, self-doubt, procrastination, addiction, distraction, timidity, ego, self-loathing, narcissism and much more.
- Resistance applies to anything you feel you want to do: anything creative; the launch of a venture; a diet or health regime; education; any act of political or moral courage

– anything that rejects immediate gratification in favour of long-term growth, health or integrity.
- Allies in doing the work are stupidity, stubbornness, blind faith, passion, assistance, and friends and family – you have to be dogged enough to carry on.
- Start before you are ready – don't over-prepare or research, just start.
- Start at the end and ask yourself: what's all this about?
- It takes balls of steel to ship – to send out the result of what you have laboured to do.

WHAT'S GOOD ABOUT IT
- Everyone needs help getting things done. Try some of these mantras:
- Stay primitive – the dafter it sounds, the better it probably is
- Trust the soup – let go of control and trust the Quantum Soup
- Be ready for resistance
- The wall is what you hit when you can't advance and there are seven principles:
  1. There is an enemy – admit it
  2. The enemy is implacable – its aim is to kill what you are doing
  3. The enemy is inside you – it's no good blaming anyone else
  4. You retain the free will to resist it
  5. The real you must duel the resistance you
  6. Resistance arises second – to neuter your dream or plan
  7. Assistance can beat resistance – how bad do you want it?

WHAT YOU HAVE TO WATCH
- Many of the examples are taken from the world of script and book writing, so you need to transfer the advice to your sphere

Drive Daniel H. Pink

WHAT THE BOOK SAYS

- Using carrots and sticks to motivate people doesn't work. We need to concentrate on autonomy, mastery and purpose.
- When it comes to motivation, there's a gap between what science knows and what business does. Our current business operating system (carrot and stick) doesn't work and often does harm.
- *Autonomy* is the desire to direct our own lives.
- *Mastery* is the urge to get better and better at something that matters.
- *Purpose* is the yearning to do what we do in the service of something larger than ourselves.
- Baseline rewards (salary, contract and a few perks) have to be adequate. Beyond that, motivation comes from autonomy, mastery and purpose.
- Type X behaviour is based on extrinsic desires such as external rewards.
- Type I behaviour is interested in intrinsic rewards – the inherent satisfaction of the activity itself (so long as baseline rewards are adequate).
- 'If-then' rewards usually do more harm than good for creative, conceptual tasks ('If you do this, then you'll get that.')
- 'Now that' rewards are offered after a task has been completed ('Now that you've done such a great job, let's acknowledge the achievement.'), and come as a surprise. These are more effective.

WHAT'S GOOD ABOUT IT

- Low-profit limited liability corporations (L3Cs) are the new breed. They operate like a for-profit business and generate a modest profit, but their primary aim is to offer social benefits.
- FedEx days (so-called because they have to deliver something overnight) allow employees to tackle any problem they want, and are hugely productive.

- People like *Goldilocks Tasks* best – not easy nor too hard. This is where people get 'in the flow' and do their best work.
- The Sawyer Effect (inspired by the Mark Twain story in which Tom persuades his friends to pay to whitewash a fence) highlights two crucial effects:
  1. Offering rewards can turn play into work (negative)
  2. Focusing on mastery can turn work into play (positive)
- A ROWE is a Results-Only Work Environment, where employees don't have schedules. They don't have to be in the office at any particular time. They just have to get their work done.

WHAT YOU HAVE TO WATCH
- Nothing. It's to the point and well-summarised so you can get straight to it.

Emotionomics DAN HILL

WHAT THE BOOK SAYS
- For too long emotions have been ignored in favour of rationality and efficiency, but breakthroughs in brain science have revealed that people are primarily emotional decision-makers.
- Companies need to catch up with this new thinking. Facial coding is the single best viable means of measuring and managing the emotional response of customers and employees.
- Science, psychology and economics now combine to move us forward: discovery of the brain's hot button (1986); articulation of emotional intelligence (1995); positive psychology movement (98); and behavioural economics (2002).
- Neurogenesis shows that new neurons are created during life, so we are not set in our ways. Mirror neurons make us mimic and empathise.

- Behavioural economics mainly covers categorisation and loss aversion:
  - *Framing:* makes a choice more attractive by deliberately comparing it with inferior options
  - *Mental accounting:* places artificial limits on what we're willing to spend
  - *Prospect theory:* judges pleasure on condition change, not how happy we are
  - *Anchoring:* evaluates new information from a base of what we already know
  - *Recency:* gives undue weight to recent experience
- Aspects of loss aversion include:
  - *Familiarity:* has a bias towards the status quo
  - *New risk premium:* inflates the cost of new risks and discounts familiar ones
  - *Fear of regret:* suffers from having to admit a mistake
  - *Decision paralysis:* fails to make one when faced with too many choices

WHAT'S GOOD ABOUT IT

- The *Facial Action Coding System* categorises the activity of 43 facial muscles. These betray four core motivations: defend, acquire, bond and learn, which dovetail with core emotions: anger, happiness, sadness, fear, disgust and surprise.
- Brand equity is emotional and is hard to measure using rational attributes. Neurons that fire together wire together – branding occurs only in the mind.
- Wundt's curve shows that maximum appeal occurs when a simple idea is presented in a novel way, or a complex idea is introduced in a familiar manner.
- Empathetic salespeople are upbeat, resilient, and, crucially, caring.
- Less than 15 per cent of US men are six foot or taller, but 58 per cent of CEOs are.

WHAT YOU HAVE TO WATCH

- It is a brilliant review of behavioural economics, but only a fraction of it is to do with facial coding.

Everything is Miscellaneous DAVID WEINBERGER

WHAT THE BOOK SAYS

- The rules of the physical world (in which everything has its place) have been upended as business, politics, science and media move online. In the digital world everything has its places (plural), with transformative effects:
  1. Information is now a social asset and should be made available for anyone to link, organise and make more valuable
  2. There's no such thing as 'too much' information – it gives people the hooks to find what they need
  3. Messiness is a digital virtue, leading to new ideas, efficiency and social knowledge
  4. Authorities are less important than buddies for trustworthy information
- Physical space puts some things nearer than others; objects can only be in one spot at a time; there is only one layout; things need to be neat.
- Information doesn't just want to be free – it wants to be miscellaneous.

WHAT'S GOOD ABOUT IT

- Atoms take up room, but content is digitised into bits. This is the third order that removes the limitations on how we organise information.
- The first order is the physical items themselves, the second is metadata (information about information – our systems for organising things).
- We have many ways to do this: nesting includes *trees* (such as genealogy) and *maps* (in which *lumps* are units of land, and *splits* are the arbitrary divisions between them).
- These days we need a *faceted classification* system that dynamically constructs a browsable, branching tree that exactly meets our needs.
- The new principles of organising information are:
  1. Filter on the way out, not on the way in
  2. Put each leaf (of data) on as many branches as possible
  3. Everything is metadata and everything can be a label

4. Give up control (let data become 'intertwingled')
- An article on Wikipedia is deemed 'neutral' when people have stopped changing it (NPOV: No Point Of View).
- Online recommendations can come unstuck: Amazon recommended books on adoption for those looking at abortion.

WHAT YOU HAVE TO WATCH
- This information is buried in dense text – you need to root it out.

Exceptional Service, Exceptional Profit
INGHILLERI & SOLOMON

WHAT THE BOOK SAYS
- Delivering brilliant service leads to higher profits via customer loyalty.
- The process only needs to be mastered once and then the rules can be applied successfully for a lifetime.
- There are five important elements:
  1. Selecting, training and inspiring loyalty virtuosos at all levels
  2. Handling service breakdowns in a systematic way that makes customers more loyal than if the mishap hadn't happened
  3. Gathering and using customer preference data
  4. Ensuring you meet customers' timeliness and quality expectations
  5. Personalising the experience of online customers
- The four main elements of customer satisfaction are perfect product, caring delivery, timeliness, and an effective problem-resolution process.
- Language engineering is important. A consistent style of speech comes from an established lexicon of preferred language and phrasing that everyone should be trained to use.

WHAT'S GOOD ABOUT IT

- If you work in a service industry you can take the examples and apply them. For example, the four steps to great service recoveries:
  1. Apologise
  2. Review the complaint with the customer
  3. Fix the problem and follow up
  4. Document it to stop it happening again
- Keeping track of customer preferences is a way to keep them coming back. You need a simple system that can be accessed in real time, but beware making assumptions because their preferences can change.
- You can work through an organisation from the leaders to the most junior staff to inculcate them with a service ethic, which affects recruitment, training and reinforcement.

WHAT YOU HAVE TO WATCH

- Not much. It's an easy read.

Hot, Flat, and Crowded THOMAS L. FRIEDMAN

WHAT THE BOOK SAYS

- It explains why the world needs a green revolution and how we can renew our global future.
- Climate change and rapid population growth mean that it's no longer possible for businesses, or the rest of us, to keep doing things the same old way. We need to change and fast. He provides a bold strategy for clean fuel, energy efficiency and conservation that he calls 'Code Green'. This is to counteract growing demand for energy and resources; the transfer of wealth to oil-rich countries; climate change; energy poverty; and accelerating biodiversity loss.
- The title is based on the fact that the world is now in danger of being hot (due to global warming), flat (due to the rise of high-consuming middle classes all over the world) and crowded (adding about a billion people every 13 years).

- He analyses when the market and Mother Nature hit the wall, showing that the parallels between the two phenomena are eerie.
- IBG (I'll be gone) and YBG (You'll be gone) refer to those exploiting people and financial markets – they won't be around to suffer the consequences. Their approach is to privatise gains and socialise loss – the taxpayer pays.
- A WWF 2008 report concluded that we are already operating 25 per cent above the planet's biological capacity to support life.
- We are the *Grasshopper Generation* – eating our way through a staggering amount of wealth and resources in a short period of time.

WHAT'S GOOD ABOUT IT
- Key the words 'world population' into Google and add the year of your birth. In 1950 there were 2.5 billion on the planet; today there are 6.8 billion, with 9 billion predicted by 2050. So in 40 years it will rise by its 1950 population.
- These are serious figures. In the last 20 years the world market has more than doubled from three to over six billion. New entrants crave the spoils previously only enjoyed by the western world, and they are getting their hands on it fast.
- From a business perspective, this certainly offers a volume opportunity in one direction, but it also means intense competitive pressure in the other.
- A huge reservoir of labour and intelligence has been released. An American can leave the office in the evening and have a presentation written overnight in India sitting on his or her desk by the morning. Geographical boundaries have in many respects disappeared where business is concerned.

WHAT YOU HAVE TO WATCH
- It is very long and detailed, so not for the faint-hearted.

Microtrends MARK J. PENN

WHAT THE BOOK SAYS

- Subtitled *Surprising tales of the way we live our lives today,* this book looks at 75 groups who, by virtue of their daily decisions, are forging the shape of America and the world.
- What they have in common is that they are relatively unseen, either because their actual numbers are small or because conventional wisdom hides their potential in the shadows, sometimes even emphasising the exact opposite.
- Among the groups he identifies are:
  - □ *Extreme commuters* – Couples that commute hundreds of miles every day or week as part of a 'normal' life
  - □ *Internet marrieds* – the large number of couples who met online
  - □ *Ardent amazons* – taller women who can handle jobs just as easily as men
  - □ *Southpaws unbound* – the increasing number of left-handers now that it is no longer such a taboo
  - □ *Late-breaking gays* – who marry women first and then change their minds
  - □ *Mildly disordered teens* – a huge percentage are on medication
  - □ *Vegan children* – and other highly demanding dietary requirements
  - □ *Shy millionaires* – those who have no splashy lifestyle but amass a lot of cash
  - □ *Uptown tattooed* – the huge increase in wealthy people having tattoos
  - □ *Video game grown-ups* – those who started playing and never stopped

WHAT'S GOOD ABOUT IT

- The book is full of chances to learn something that would make good dinner table conversation.
- Strange factoids include:
  1. There are more Christian Zionists than Jewish ones

2. One percent of young Californians want to grow up to be military snipers
3. As a result of the crime crackdown, one of the fastest-growing population segments is newly released ex-convicts
4. Knitting is experiencing a revival among young people
5. Those who love technology are more outgoing than those who hate technology

- In the brief concluding section there's an effort to pull it all together: in a world with more choices, people will fragment in their selections (*The Long Tail* already told us this).

WHAT YOU HAVE TO WATCH
- There's not much analysis of products or positions that such groups might like.

Obliquity JOHN KAY

WHAT THE BOOK SAYS
- Paradoxically, many goals are more likely to be achieved when pursued indirectly. The most profitable companies are not the most aggressive in chasing profits, the wealthiest people are not the most materialistic, and the happiest people do not pursue happiness. This is the concept of 'obliquity'.
- The profit-seeking paradox echoes Collins & Porras in *Built to Last:* the most successful companies did not put profit first.
- Oblique approaches often take a step back to move forward. Apparently daunting tasks are made easier by doing *something,* and then learning. This approach is often more fruitful than laboriously detailed planning.
- This is what Charles Lindblom described as *The Science of Muddling Through.*
- Direct approaches are often impracticable because the world is too complex, so problem-solving needs to be iterative and adaptive.

WHAT'S GOOD ABOUT IT

- The differences between direct and oblique approaches are instructive:

  1. *Loosely defined and multi-dimensional objectives*
     v. Objectives that are clear, and can be defined and quantified

  2. *No clear distinction between goals and actions*
     v. A clear distinction between goals and actions, and how to achieve them

  3. *Actions and context influence next action*
     v. Interactions with others are limited

  4. *Imperfect knowledge, learnt on the way*
     v. Structure of relationships clearly understood

  5. *Only a limited number of options identified or perceived as available*
     v. Range of options, fixed and known

  6. *Outcomes arise through complex processes no one fully grasps*
     v. What happens is what we intend to happen

  7. *Recognise that only limited knowledge is available*
     v. Decisions made on the basis of the fullest possible information

  8. *Good outcomes derived through continual, often unsuccessful, adaptation*
     v. Best outcomes through a conscious process of maximisation

- Judgements about feelings, rather than the feelings themselves, explain why we do things that involve hardship, such as parenthood or mountaineering.

- Decision-making models are not used to inform decision-making, but to justify decisions that have already been made.

- Compare the world to a game of Sudoku: there is only one solution; we know when we have found it; play is not influenced by the responses of others; there is a complete list of possible actions; and complexity has a limit. But human brains work on real problems, not artificial ones, and obliquity works best.

WHAT YOU HAVE TO WATCH
- It is a relatively complicated read, but worth the effort.

On Bullshit HARRY G. FRANKFURT

WHAT THE BOOK SAYS
- The author is a professor at Princeton University and a renowned moral philosopher. This is a thoughtful debate on an unusual subject for academia.
- Bullshit is now ubiquitous, but strangely has not attracted much sustained inquiry because we think we know how to spot it and deal with it.
- It is not easy to define because the term is often used loosely and as a generic term of abuse – it covers a multitude of sins.
- Synonyms for humbug suggested by Max Black (1985) include balderdash, buncombe, claptrap, drivel, hokum, imposture and quackery.
- Constituent elements of it are deceptive misrepresentation, short of lying, especially by pretentious word or deed, and misrepresentation of somebody's own thoughts, feelings or attitudes.
- Frankfurt deconstructs these elements and compares bullshit to shoddy goods – produced in a careless or self-indulgent manner, and never finely crafted.
- The essence of bullshit is a lack of concern with the truth and an indifference to how things really are. It involves a kind of bluff.
- Does the bullshitter lie? Not necessarily. He is phony rather than false. The bullshitter is faking things, but this does not mean that he necessarily gets them wrong. As such, he has much more freedom than someone who tells the truth or lies, because they do not require an anchor point on one side or the other.
- The production of bullshit is stimulated whenever a person's obligations or opportunities to speak about something exceed his knowledge of the facts that are relevant to the topic.

WHAT'S GOOD ABOUT IT

- *'The realms of advertising and of public relations, and the nowadays closely related realm of politics, are replete with instances of bullshit so unmitigated that they can serve among the most indisputable and classic paradigms of the concept.'*
- *'The truth-values of (the bullshitter's) statements are of no central interest to him; what we are not to understand is that his intention is neither to report the truth nor to conceal it.'*
- *'He is neither on the side of the truth nor on the side of the false.'*
- *'He does not care whether the things he says describe reality correctly. He just picks them out, or makes them up, to suit his purpose.'*
- *'He does not reject the authority of truth, as the liar does, and oppose himself to it. He pays no attention to it at all.'*

WHAT YOU HAVE TO WATCH

- This is an academic essay, not a 'pop' book, so you need to concentrate on the line of argument carefully, but you can read it in an hour, which helps.

Poke the Box SETH GODIN

WHAT THE BOOK SAYS

- It is subtitled: *When was the last time you did something for the first time?*
- It is a manifesto about starting things, making a ruckus, and taking what feels like a risk.
- A buzzer box has some lights and switches on it – when you poke it, things happen. When I do this, what happens?; What can you start?; Soon is not as good as now.
- When the cost of poking the box is less than the cost of doing nothing, then you should poke. Poking isn't about being right. It means action.
- He outlines seven imperatives:

1. Be aware – of the market, opportunities, and who you are
2. Be educated – so you can understand what is around you
3. Be connected – so you can be trusted as you engage
4. Be consistent – so the system knows what to expect
5. Build an asset – so you have something to sell
6. Be productive – so you can be well-priced
7. Have the guts and heart and passion to ship (get it out of the door)

- Human nature is to need a map. Stop waiting for one. If you're brave enough to draw one, people will follow. The challenge is getting into the habit of starting.
- Anxiety is experiencing failure in advance. If you are anxious about starting a project, then you will associate risk with failure. Starting means you're going to finish.

WHAT'S GOOD ABOUT IT

- This is a call to arms. What could you build?
- Followers want to be picked for promotion, praise, or some other credit. They are saying: 'Pick me!'. You should reject the tyranny of 'picked' and pick yourself.
- Excellence isn't about working extra hard to do what you're told. It's about taking the initiative to do work you decide is worth doing.
- 'This might not work' is a healthy approach. Focus on the work, not the fear that comes from doing the work. The person who fails the most usually wins.
- Juggling is about throwing, not catching. If you get better at throwing, the catches take care of themselves.
- The Dandelion Mind idea is engaging: dandelions produce 2,000 seeds a year and it doesn't matter where they land. Produce a lot and things will happen.

WHAT YOU HAVE TO WATCH

- Nothing. This is a motivating rallying call.

Predictably Irrational DAN ARIELY

WHAT THE BOOK SAYS

- Subtitled *The Hidden Forces that Shape Our Decisions,* the book explains how to break through our systematic patterns of thought to make better, more financially sound, decisions.
- We think we are in control when it comes to making decisions, but are we? A series of experiments reveal the truth: expectations, emotions, social norms and other invisible, seemingly illogical forces skew our reasoning abilities.
- We make astonishingly simple mistakes, and usually the same type:
  1. *Consistently overpaying, underestimating and procrastinating*
  2. *Failing to understand the effects of emotions on what we want*
  3. *Overvaluing what we already own*
- The good news is that these misguided behaviours are neither random nor senseless. They're systematic and predictable – hence the title.

WHAT'S GOOD ABOUT IT

- This book is a close cousin of *Freakonomics, Nudge, Sway* and several other books on behavioural economics, the study of the financial implications of the judgements and decisions we make. The promise of the discipline is to learn to take into account our flaws and inabilities when we design our world, and thus make it a better place. And yet its greatest challenge is demonstrating its applicability in the real world.
- *'In theory, there is no difference between theory and practice, but in practice there is a great deal of difference.'* Al Roth, Harvard economist.
- The author is a social scientist with a crucial life story that leads to an observational perspective – aged 18 he was blown up by a magnesium flare in Israel and suffered third-degree burns on 70 per cent of his body.

- Measures we can grapple with include:
  1. *Everything is relative: decoy effects fool us into thinking otherwise*
  2. *Supply and demand links are often a fallacy: beware being imprinted into thinking something is more desirable than it truly is*
  3. *Arbitrary coherence is common: for example, just thinking about old people can make you walk slower*
  4. *Self-herding is habitual behaviour that you create yourself: it can make you do daft things*
  5. *The Tom Sawyer principle means that some people will pay you to do something when the transaction should have been the other way round (in the story he manages to get his friends to pay him for the privilege of whitewashing his aunt's fence)*
  6. *Free is a confusing concept that makes us go for things we don't really want*
  7. *You can't mix social and market norms: you don't offer to pay for the meal that your mother cooks you, and companies can't have it both ways*

WHAT YOU HAVE TO WATCH
- Not much. It rolls along nicely and makes the points in a clear way.

Predicting Market Success ROBERT PASSIKOFF

WHAT THE BOOK SAYS
- Brand success is the degree to which the brand meets or exceeds what consumers want, need and expect in the category, both emotionally and rationally.
- Brands that do that have equity. Brands that don't have problems.
- The technique, the book explains, is to evaluate Brands (what already exists in the present) against the Ideal (what consumers wish existed in the future).
- This generates a consumer-centric view of the category in which the brand competes, letting it understand how

consumers view, compare, and choose among category options.
- As such this is a predictive solution rather than a historical one. It can easily be integrated into current research efforts, and can demonstrate Brand Equity ROI, quantifying the impact of marketing initiatives in advance of spend.
- It is effectively a loyalty-based customer listening system that claims to outperform traditional research methods.
- Today's purchasing decisions are 70 per cent emotional, so there's a big difference between what consumers say they want and what they end up buying.
- As such, the old model of product, place, price and promotion has been replaced with customer engagement, expectations and loyalty.

WHAT'S GOOD ABOUT IT
- Research tells you little until you examine the category drivers, their vital components, their order of importance, what expectations people have of them, and how your brand stacks up against all of those. Even worse, they are changing all the time and need to be measured regularly.
- Then you can plot your brand against category expectations and quantify the gap between what people want and what your brand is actually delivering. For example, your brand rating could go up, but category expectations might go up even further, thus increasing the gap. Only looking at the former figure will provide false optimism for the brand owner, and lead to falling sales.
- Consumer expectations are up 28 per cent on average, so keeping pace with what they really want is crucial, and yet 85 per cent of new products fail.
- People knowing a brand (awareness), or even loving it (admiration), is not the same as using it (purchase). Measuring the wrong part is misleading.
- Plenty of companies use 'important-sounding but resonance-free' offerings as a basis for brand success.

WHAT YOU HAVE TO WATCH
- The layout is pretty traditional, but there is flowing prose within. Beware if graphs scare you, because there are lots of them.

Revolution BILL LUCAS

WHAT THE BOOK SAYS
- To survive our current crazy world we need a new kind of mind-ware – ways to develop our adaptive intelligence. One hundred and fifty years after Charles Darwin invented the concept of natural selection, the rules of evolution are changing, with the speed of change accelerating faster than ever.
- Mind-ware consists of personal habits of mind and patterns of social interaction.
- We all need to become better at dealing with crazy amounts of information. Too much choice makes us unhappy. Learners inherit the earth, while the learned are beautifully equipped to deal with a world that no longer exists.
- We need to explore the unlearning curve: how quickly can we unlearn?
- Visible thinking encourages a tangible response to new stimuli: what's going on here and what do I see that makes me say so?
- Unfreeze/move/refreeze summarises the change process. It's not the changes that do you in, it's the transitions.
- How we see the world depends on:
  - *Permanence:* pessimists think it's fixed, optimists move on
  - *Personalisation:* pessimists blame themselves, optimists get round things
  - *Pervasiveness:* pessimists let setbacks spread, optimists see isolated incidents

WHAT'S GOOD ABOUT IT

- There are nine rules to work with:
  1. *Change is changing:* it is no longer gradual. We need to cultivate habits of mind associated with imagining, noticing, choosing, synthesising and unlearning
  2. *Real change is internal:* instead of looking at the outside world, we should look to letting go, noticing and naming emotions, and the development of resilience
  3. *Slow down:* being, deferring, surfacing and reflecting are helpful qualities here
  4. *We can all change the way we see the world:* personality and events are not fixed and inevitable.
  5. *We can learn how to change more effectively:* adaptive intelligence holds the key
  6. *No one can make you change:* we don't have to follow the herd
  7. *Sometimes it's smart to resist:* not all change is helpful
  8. *Use the brainpower of those around you:* sociability and working together
  9. *Make up your own rules:* find your own style and go with it
- The PDSA cycle is crucial: plan, do, study, act (with study being crucial).
- Classifying issues as plus, minus, interesting helps solve tricky ones.

WHAT YOU HAVE TO WATCH

- It is a great synthesis for coping with life but you may have seen a lot of the ideas elsewhere.

Rework FRIED & HANSSON

WHAT THE BOOK SAYS

- Most of what you are told about building, running and growing a business is nonsense. You can change the way you work forever by ignoring most conventions from normal companies.

- The book doesn't really have chapters. Instead it has ultra-short sections with pithy pieces of advice, and there are lots of them, including:
  1. Ignore the real world – people who say something won't work are often wrong
  2. Learn from your successes, not your failures
  3. Planning is guessing – have a go and get on with it
  4. Why grow? Being a large business may be pointless and counterproductive
  5. Workaholism is for fools – you don't have to be that busy to succeed
  6. Enough with 'entrepreneurs' – let's just call them starters
  7. Make a dent in the universe – try to change something
  8. Scratch your own itch – do something you want to do
  9. Start making something – no time is no excuse
  10. Outside money is plan Z – don't borrow if you don't have to
  11. Embrace constraints – they make your work more specific
  12. Throw less at the problem – do less, better
  13. Sell your by-products – the stuff you reject on the way may have value too
  14. Meetings are toxic – have as few as possible
  15. Good enough is fine – get something underway and fix it as you go
  16. Long lists don't get done – make tiny decisions and see the progress
  17. Don't confuse enthusiasm with priority

WHAT'S GOOD ABOUT IT

- The gems keep coming: ASAP is poison, underdo the competition, inspiration is perishable – fight bloat and fire the workaholics.
- You could dip into this book anywhere and grab a motivating thought on anything from launching to hiring, productivity to promotion.

WHAT YOU HAVE TO WATCH
- Nothing. It's great.

Smart Swarm PETER MILLER

WHAT THE BOOK SAYS
- Understanding how flocks, schools and colonies work can make us better at communicating, decision-making and getting things done.
- Studying the collective intelligence of ants, bees, termites, birds, fish, and locusts can give us great ideas for solving business and social problems. Many of them have already been adopted by the worlds of finance, the military and even Google.
- The major principles of a smart swarm are:
  1. *Self-organisation* – this is made up of decentralised control (nobody's in charge); distributed problem-solving (each individual sorts something out); and multiple interactions (lots of individuals paying attention to what the other is doing)
  2. *Diversity of knowledge* – when many bees head in different directions looking for honey, they increase the hive's collective chance of finding it
  3. *Indirect collaboration* – in a process sometimes called stigmergy, termites follow a simple rule of 'drop your grain of sand here if somebody else has already done so'. The collaboration is indirect because they do not have to interact with a colleague for this to occur, and the communication is achieved indirectly by modifying the environment
  4. *Adaptive mimicking* – coordination, communication and copying can unleash powerful waves of energy in a collective population

WHAT'S GOOD ABOUT IT
- Amplifying success is a helpful concept. The more ants take the shortest path, the more continue to do so, thus

increasing efficiency. This can be emulated in the business world.
- Swarm lessons are salutary:
  - seek a diversity of knowledge
  - encourage a friendly competition of ideas
  - use an effective mechanism to narrow your choices
- Many businesses are like a complex adaptive organism without a central nervous system, with units operating in silos and not sharing knowledge.
- It is proven that groups of three or four people perform better than the best individual because their sum total of problem-solving skills is greater.

WHAT YOU HAVE TO WATCH
- It is not laid out like a business book with easy captions in bold – you have to dig for these findings, but it's worth it.

Socialnomics Erik Qualman

WHAT THE BOOK SAYS
- Social media is transforming the way we live and do business. This is a massive socio-economic shift that is fundamentally changing the way consumers and companies communicate with each other.
- Traditional marketing strategies are obsolete, and have been replaced by Socialnomics, where online communities influence companies and markets.
- Brands can now be strengthened or destroyed by social media. Advertising is less effective. Companies and customers can now connect direct.
- Word of mouth is now World of mouth – international instantly.
- Social media provides a preventative role: what happens in Vegas now stays on YouTube.
- It also increases efficiency by eliminating multiple individual redundancies.
- On the downside, it facilitates braggadocian behaviour – self-centred, 'it's all about me'. Another drawback is an

erosion of confidence in meeting and communicating with people in person: 'the next generation can't speak'.
- The old adage that you can only have two out of three of cheap, quick or quality isn't true in social media – you can have all three because someone may already have done part of it for you.

WHAT'S GOOD ABOUT IT
- He defines Socialommerce, in which billions of dollars will be made in and around social media.
- People don't care what Google thinks, they care what their peers and neighbours think.
- Schizophrenic behaviour, in which individuals and companies have different work and play personalities, will disappear as they become the same thing.
- Bacon salt was invented by two guys in Seattle who ran an online survey asking who would like a powder that made everything taste like bacon. They found a market before they hade invented the product.
- Apple have hired a 22-year-old who has never sent an email. He has always used instant message, text, phone or social media.
- An 83-year-old prints out his social media updates to find out what is contributing to a full life. On discovering any 'unfruitful activities', he ceases them immediately.

WHAT YOU HAVE TO WATCH
- Not much. It makes lots of interesting points and summarises clearly at then end of each chapter.

Sticky Wisdom MATT KINGDON ET AL.

WHAT THE BOOK SAYS
- You can start a creative revolution at work by thinking and behaving differently. The secret lies in simple, practical learning about how creativity works.
- The authors set up arguably the first innovation company in the United Kingdom called *What If?* The book outlines their philosophy and explains a process, and related

workshops and exercises that allow you to follow their approach.
- It is something of a call to arms – encouraging companies to manage the human mind more effectively, to add value and uniqueness to what they do, and to liberate creativity and innovation.

WHAT'S GOOD ABOUT IT

- You can easily follow the techniques for being more creative. They are:
  1. *Freshness:* the quality of the initial stimulus has a direct bearing on how good the final ideas are. (River jumping exercises here include re-expression, looking at related worlds, revolution via challenging assumptions, and making random links)*
  2. *Greenhousing:* young ideas need protection when they are at their most vulnerable. (SUN = Suspend judgement + Understand + Nurture, RAIN = React + Assume + Insist – this will kill most ideas immediately)
  3. *Realness:* once you stop talking and start doing you can make real progress. (Bring the idea to life very early rather than keep talking about it)
  4. *Momentum:* you need to dismantle barriers and generate 'unreasonable urgency'. (Seek alignment, create crisis, say no to distractions)
  5. *Signalling:* an enabling characteristic that strengthens and sustains ideas. (Navigate between the analytical and creative world, Tune in + Choose to act + Propose a response)
  6. *Courage:* overcoming mediocrity and being brave. (Show your struggle, stretch your comfort zone, get convicted)

WHAT YOU HAVE TO WATCH

- It's a book but it's also very much a brochure for the company.
- The title of the original book was *What If?*, which seems more relevant than *Sticky Wisdom* (this barely gets a mention in the body of the book).

*Many of these exercises are similar to those in other books, such as Adam Morgan's *Eating the Big Fish* (re-expression/reframing); *The Brand Innovation Manifesto* by John Grant (related worlds/category stealing); and Wayne Lotherington's *Flicking your Creative Switch* (random links/ random word). That's not a crime, but it's worth being aware of the connections.

The Business Playground Dave Stewart & Mark Simmons

WHAT THE BOOK SAYS

- Grown-ups can rediscover the magic of creativity that we all had as children, and apply it to business, but most people 'unlearn' how to do it.
- Creative brilliance is possible when we allow ourselves to move outside the expected, whereas education and work stifle our natural creative talents.
- Having lots of ideas increases the likelihood that some will be good – 'idea spaghetti'.
- Not accepting the status quo is a good starting point for innovation. It's important to be constantly curious and looking for things to improve. What bugs you most about something? Now work out how to improve it.
- Asking the right questions increases the chances of finding the right solutions – 'the answer is in the question'. Assumptions need to be scrutinised.
- Taking your mind off solving a problem increases your chance of solving it.
- Visualising ideas helps free up creative thinking, but evocative language also helps. So does taking time with the details so they are as vivid as possible.
- Thinking big helps, as does trying on other people's shoes, and using orchestrated chaos. Others will certainly see things differently to you.
- You need to murder any ideas that aren't worth spending time on, and then choose the big one and put it into orbit.

WHAT'S GOOD ABOUT IT

- There are lots of techniques and games to help train your creative muscles.
- Creativity and commerce can collide to great effect if we allow ourselves to free up proper play-based thinking.
- Convergent thinking converges on one single answer, whereas divergent thinking has many possible answers – this is likely to be more fruitful.
- The brain prepares itself to come up with an insight even before it has solved the problem – it's fine to relax into this process and let it happen naturally.
- Ignore the most obvious creative solutions or put them to one side. Creativity is about making connections between two seemingly unconnected things.

WHAT YOU HAVE TO WATCH

- Having Dave Stewart of Eurythmics fame as a co-author is initially appealing, but in fact he just adds an anecdote at the end of each chapter.
- A fair number of the exercises aren't original –they can be found in other books such as *Flicking Your Creative Switch.*

The Great Stagnation TYLER COWEN

WHAT THE BOOK SAYS

- The snappy subtitle of this medium-length e-book is *How America Ate All the Low-Hanging Fruit of Modern History, Got Sick, and Will (Eventually) Recover.*
- The overall line of argument is that most of the things that generated economic growth have now been used up (the low-hanging fruit), certainly from a US perspective. We need to get used to this to have a more realistic view of how economies can work and what they can afford.
- The LHF that America 'ate' was all the free land, the quantity of technological breakthroughs, and improved education that fuelled growth. This lasted about 300 years but has now mostly gone.

- Most developed countries have seen their economic growth slowing since the 1970s because technological development has slowed.
- It was easier for the average person to produce an important innovation in the nineteenth century than in the twentieth. This means a lower and declining rate of return on technology.
- A lot of our recent innovations are 'private goods' rather than 'public goods' – they have made a few individuals very wealthy but do not translate to gains for the average citizen.

WHAT'S GOOD ABOUT IT

- The theory is interesting: when you combine three macroeconomic events – growing income inequality, stagnant median income, and the financial crisis – you can see why our 'new economy' is not as productive as before.
- Productivity figures that rise can be misleading. For example, the biggest gain in the last few years has been discovering who isn't producing very much and firing them.
- Although the Internet is highly innovative, it doesn't generate nearly as many jobs or as much income as traditional businesses. Google has 20,000 employees and eBay 16,400, but Facebook has only 1,700 and Twitter 300. The Internet is great because it gives us 'cheap fun' but it's not generating the scale of revenue necessary to replace what we've lost.
- Cowen's recommendation is to raise the social status of scientists, so that we fuel more ideas that generate growth.
- Other than that, 'we are living in the new normal'.

WHAT YOU HAVE TO WATCH

- This is an e-book so you need a Kindle or iPad to get it, and need to be comfortable with that reading format. On the plus side, this enables the author to keep it shorter than an average book – more of an extended essay – so he doesn't go on longer than he needs to in order to make the point.

The Language Wars HENRY HITCHINGS

WHAT THE BOOK SAYS

- This book unpacks how the history of 'proper' English came about. It looks at grammar rules, regional accents, swearing, spelling, dictionaries, political correctness and the role of electronic media in reshaping language.
- People get angry about English, arguing about slang, abbreviations, buzzwords (itself a buzzword?), vocabulary imported from other languages, the abuse of apostrophes, and the mistakes of public figures who 'ought to know better'.
- But people have always worried about the state of English, from Chaucer through to Dickens and Shakespeare to the modern day.
- Rules are a sort of armour, and yet rule-makers miss out on the dynamism of speech. Rules are really mental mechanisms that carry out operations to combine words in helpful arrangements so we can be understood.
- The author is not arguing that there should be no norms or rules, just that we ought to think beyond tradition, habit and deference, and to consider what we want from our words.
- We need to engage with language – we tend to discuss it in a cantankerous or petulant way, but thinking and talking about it should be a pleasure.

WHAT'S GOOD ABOUT IT

- This is a series of 28 pithy essays that guide us through the history of our language, from slang and spelling to text messaging.
- Given the recent rise of English as the world's default Internet language, it is important that we look at it carefully and understand it.

- We all have our pet hates, but these start to look rather foolish if you take the long view.
- Jonathan Swift hated the words 'mob' and 'banter'. Dr Johnson hated 'trait' and 'ruse', mainly because they were French in origin. Not long ago 'mileage' and 'hindsight' were regarded as awful Americanisms. Things move on.
- Complaints about English are as old as the hills, based on no linguistic logic and are fairly futile, since no one can stop language from evolving, and it is healthy that it does.
- The reader can either regard this as a call to arms, or just a pleasant ramble through the vagaries of our strange language.

WHAT YOU HAVE TO WATCH
- It is fairly long and very detailed, and so is not for the faint-hearted. However, being broken down into 28 essays, it can be cherry-picked.

The Little Big Things TOM PETERS
WHAT THE BOOK SAYS
- This is not a book with a cohesive theme in the traditional sense – it contains 163 ways to pursue excellence that were originally a series of blogs.
- It's the soft things that matter, and they are very hard to do.
- Hundreds of small acts of humanity add up to big improvements in operational effectiveness.
- Behavioural economics tallies with irrationality, and that often means dramatic overreaction to some tiny thing, or under reaction to a big thing.
- The characteristic that can help us when dealing with random events (Black Swans) is resilience, usually demonstrated by people with inner calm, high self-knowledge and a sense of humour.
- Big change really can be achieved in a short space of time – it will take precisely as long as you think it will.
- Big plans don't work – small steps get things done.

- Planners announce good intentions but don't motivate anyone to carry them out. Searchers find things that work and build on them.
- Serious play beats serious planning – all practical ideas evolve from prototypes.

WHAT'S GOOD ABOUT IT
- Seth Godin says that if you can't describe your position in eight words or less, you don't have a position. Peters call this an RPOV (Remarkable Point Of View). All businesses, and people, should have one.
- Kindness is free, so deploy it more often.
- To Don't lists are often more important than To Do lists – over half of what we do is unnecessary.
- Leaders should practice Servant Leadership: what did I specifically do today to be of service to my people?
- Staff are a more important audience than the customer – if they are not happy and motivated, then the customer won't be either, so it starts on the inside.
- Apology is one of the most powerful tools at anyone's disposal.
- Don't learn from your failures – look for things that went right and build on them.

WHAT YOU HAVE TO WATCH
- The book is riddled with exclamation marks (over 60 on the inside cover and contents pages alone), which will prove irritating to those who favour a more sedate approach.
- There is a lot of repetition to the point where it feels there is much less in it than the large format suggests. It could probably be edited down to less than half the size.

The Living Company ARIE DE GEUS

WHAT THE BOOK SAYS
- What if we thought about a company as a living being, rather than just a series of monetary assets?

- Seeing a company as a machine implies that it is fixed, that it will eventually run down, and that its people are straightforward (human) resources.
- Living companies evolve naturally because people generate change, they regenerate naturally, and can learn as entities.
- Living companies have four components:
  - *Learning:* sensitivity to the environment and an ability to learn and adapt
  - *Persona:* cohesion and identity as aspects of an innate ability to build a community
  - *Ecology:* tolerance, decentralisation, and an ability to build relationships with other entities
  - *Evolution:* ability to govern its own growth effectively, including conservative finance
- The average company lifespan is 40 years, with humans lasting 70. They die early because the thinking and language of management are too narrowly based on economics. They forget that their organisation's true nature is that of a community of humans.

WHAT'S GOOD ABOUT IT
- Possible reasons why managers fail include:
  - managers are stupid (he does not believe this);
  - we can only see when a crisis opens our eyes;
  - we can only see what we have already experienced;
  - we cannot see what is emotionally difficult to see;
  - we can only see what is relevant to our view of the future.
- This is all based on what the Swedish neurobiologist David Ingvar calls a 'memory of the future', in which we have envisaged a series of scenarios. Usually 60 per cent are positive and 40 per cent negative, but if the balance is disturbed, then incorrigible optimists or pessimists take centre stage.
- In the 1930s the corporate world tried to address this with 'tools for foresight' – the dreaded strategic planning that creates the illusion of certainty where there is none.

- Most companies learn through Perceiving, Embedding, Concluding and Acting.

WHAT YOU HAVE TO WATCH

- The author spent his entire career at Shell, so all the examples come from there.

The Paradox of Choice BARRY SCHWARTZ

WHAT THE BOOK SAYS

- It is subtitled *Why more is less,* and explains how the culture of abundance robs us of satisfaction. The author argues that we would be better off if we embraced voluntary constraints and sought what was 'good enough' instead of seeking the best. To reduce stress, we should lower our expectations, make our decisions non-reversible and pay less attention to what others are doing.
- Negative liberty is freedom from (constraint) and positive liberty is freedom to (do what we want).
- The more choice we have, the less we actually make decisions – the tyranny of small decisions paralyses us.
- Choices are based on expected and remembered utility – how people felt when the experience was at its peak (best or worst) and at the end. The psychologist Daniel Kahneman calls this the peak-end rule.
- Kahneman & Tversky, revered behavioural economists, defined the availability heuristic, in which people give undue weight to some types of information in relation to others, leading to irrational decisions.
- Prospect theory suggests that evaluations are relative to a baseline – a hedonic zero point that determines whether something appears 'better' or 'worse'.

WHAT'S GOOD ABOUT IT

- Maximizers consider every possibility, are always wondering what the other options are, and are never satisfied. Too much choice increases their stress.

- Perfectionists set high standards they don't expect to meet, but maximizers do expect to meet them, and are disappointed when they don't.
- Satisficers are happy with 'good enough' and have few regrets.
- Learned helplessness assumes that it won't work so there's no point trying.
- Opportunity costs are missing the opportunities afforded by a different option.
- If we want to cope better with choice we need to choose when to choose; be a chooser not a picker; satisfice more and maximize less; think about the opportunity costs of opportunity costs; make decisions non-reversible; practice an attitude of gratitude; regret less; anticipate adaptation; control expectations; curtail social comparison; and learn to love constraints.

WHAT YOU HAVE TO WATCH
- This is a highly readable and thought-provoking book, and should be read by anyone with an interest in behavioural economics.

The Rules of Management RICHARD TEMPLAR

WHAT THE BOOK SAYS
- Described as a definitive code for managerial success, this book provides 100 rules – a blend of serious advice tinged with a fair dollop of cynicism. It is divided into managing your team and managing yourself.
- Managing your team points include:
  - □ *Get them emotionally involved (many manage aloofly)*
  - □ *Set realistic targets (how often does this happen?)*
  - □ *Hold effective meetings (when were you last in one of these?)*
  - □ *Offload as much as you can – or dare (the art of delegation)*
  - □ *Be ready to prune (this is the tough bit)*
  - □ *Take the rap (even tougher)*

- □ *Be ready to say 'yes' (others think saying no is equally important)*
- Managing yourself points include:
  - □ *Have a game plan, but keep it secret (a bit odd this – most would publicise it)*
  - □ *Be consistent (how many managers change their minds all the time?)*
  - □ *Get rid of superfluous rules (slightly ironic in a book that offers 100 of them)*
  - □ *Learn from your mistakes (as opposed to repeating the same ineffective stuff)*
  - □ *Manage your health (do you have a stressed-out boss?)*
  - □ *Don't stagnate (hanging frantically on to a job is bad for all)*
- You can immediately see the potential conflict between being a wonderful person and being an effective boss. Arguably, no book has ever resolved this.
- Managing effectively involves three choices: put up with it, change it or end it.

WHAT'S GOOD ABOUT IT

- *'Getting good players is easy. Getting them to play together is the hard part.'* Casey Stengel, New York Yankees manager
- *'The ideas that come out of brainstorming sessions are usually superficial, trivial, and not very original. They are rarely useful. The process, however, seems to make uncreative people feel that they are making innovative contributions and that others are listening to them.'* A. Harvey Block
- *'It is amazing how much you can accomplish if you do not care who gets the credit.'* Harry Truman
- *'It's a very difficult job and the only way through is that we all work together as a team. And that means you do everything I say.'* Michael Caine, *The Italian Job*

WHAT YOU HAVE TO WATCH

- As ever, it is usually easier to suggest these things than actually enact them.

The Spirit Level Delusion CHRISTOPHER SNOWDON

WHAT THE BOOK SAYS

- A number of books, including *The Sprit Level, Affluenza* and *The Selfish Capitalist,* have made extraordinary claims in favour of big government, calling for a radical shift in power from the individual to the state.
- The claims they make are based on the supposedly devastating effects of wealth, economic growth and inequality, but this book shows that the theory not only lacks empirical support but also fails the basic test of believability.
- The original *Spirit Level* authors, Wilkinson & Pickett, believe that more equal societies do better, and try to prove the point by showing higher rates of suicide, crime, mental illness and infant mortality (and lower rates of happiness) in unequal ones.
- *The Spirit Level Delusion* works methodically through all these claims, and pretty much discredits every one of them.
- Mixed methodologies and pick 'n' mix data are major culprits – Wilkinson & Pickett effectively only choose the bits that suit them.
- All anti-consumerist tracts end up recommending higher taxes, more government and fresh prohibition, regardless of where they start: mental health (*Affluenza* – Oliver James); shopping (*All Consuming* – Neal Lawson); health (*Status Syndrome* – Michael Marmot); or quality of life (*Happiness* – Richard Layard).

WHAT'S GOOD ABOUT IT

- The book contains no big idea. Instead, it is a careful look at the data.
- It concludes only that we live in a complex world of infinite subtleties and variation, and that the future lies in improving material conditions for all rather than forcibly protecting individuals from their own emotions.

- Status anxiety exists, but is overstated. Only an advocate of the psychosocial theory would suggest that seeing the bigger seats when leaving an aircraft created the difference between flying economy or first class, rather than the more obvious tangible benefits.
- Snowdon's dismantling of the evidence makes for great reading. To illustrate the daftness of some of the causations supposedly drawn, he produces a thoroughly plausible graph to show the correlation between educational achievement and proximity to the North Pole.
- Other comments include *'this mind-boggling combination of rhetorical tricks and non sequiturs suggests an unfulfilled career as a defence lawyer.'*

WHAT YOU HAVE TO WATCH
- It tries to be neutral, but it is a response with a stance, so you have to aim off for that.

The Undercover Economist TIM HARFORD

WHAT THE BOOK SAYS
- This book claims to offer the hidden story behind the forces that shape our everyday lives – it's like spending the day wearing x-ray goggles and suddenly understanding the economic incentive that drives everything.
- In theory, economics can illuminate every aspect of the world we inhabit – if it is explained clearly enough.
- This covers, among other things, why the gap between rich and poor nations is so great, why it's so difficult to get a foot on the property ladder, or why you can't buy a decent second-hand car.
- Supermarkets have price targeting down to a fine art: walk 500 metres in Liverpool Street and you can save 15 per cent on pretty much everything. Coffee shops are the same, but who would walk that distance to save 30p?
- Price targeting in products goes to extremes: IBM have to put an additional chip in their low-end printer to slow it down and justify the lower price.

- Pricing strategies encounter snags when they 'leak'
  – either when rich customers buy cheap products, or when
  products leak from one group to another.
- Group price targeting is inefficient because it takes
  products away from customers who are willing to pay
  more, and gives them to those who pay less.

WHAT'S GOOD ABOUT IT
- Perfectly competitive markets result in four main
  components:
  1. *Companies who make things the right way*
  2. *Companies who make the right things*
  3. *Things that are made in the right proportions*
  4. *Things that are going to the 'right' people*
- Some markets suffer from asymmetric information, where
  one negotiator knows more than the other. With second-
  hand cars, people won't pay over the odds for one that
  has a 50/50 chance of being a peach rather than a lemon.
- Equally, insurance policies are based on mutual ignorance
  – neither side knows what will happen.
- Smart, diligent people can prove they are just that by
  going to the trouble of getting a degree, and employers
  will pay them accordingly.

WHAT YOU HAVE TO WATCH
- Compared to other economist writing, this is a breeze, and
  flows along nicely. However, in relation to bite-size
  business writing, it remains fairly heavy duty. Towards the
  end, the economist's perspective can wane somewhat.

Think! EDWARD DE BONO

WHAT THE BOOK SAYS
- Our current way of thinking is not good enough, and
  here's what we can do about it.
- While our methods are excellent when applied to science
  and technology, when we attempt to tackle more human
  issues like climate change and war, we make no progress
  at all.

- **PO stands for Provocative Operation, and can also be linked to possible, hypothesis, pose, potential, etc. Interjected into conversations, PO has the power to push thinking along faster and more productively.**
- **Operacy is as important as literacy and numeracy. It's the skill of operating or getting things done, but schools only concentrate on the first two.**
- **There are many types of important thinking:**
  - □ *Perceptual thinking* **is more powerful than logic in changing behaviour**
  - □ *Exploratory thinking* **is more likely to achieve progress than argument**
  - □ *Critical thinking,* **as espoused by the Greek Gang of Three (Socrates, Plato and Aristotle), is excellent but not enough. It is fine for destroying ideas but not for creating new ideas in the first place.**

WHAT'S GOOD ABOUT IT

- **He argues that those who claim that the term 'problem-solving' covers everything suggest that 'anything you want to do' forms a problem, which includes any mental activity. This is misleading and dangerous because it excludes all other forms of thinking.**
- **The Septine is a new concept in which you write down seven different thoughts about a situation. There is no logical sequence and it is not analysis. They are merely scattered elements that could lead to better thoughts.**
- **In business there is an obvious need for new thinking, because you can argue till you are blue in the face that you are right, and still go bankrupt a month later.**
- **A 'proto-truth' describes something we hold to be true, providing we are trying to change it. This can be more creatively fruitful than the belief that we already have the true answer.**

WHAT YOU HAVE TO WATCH

- **As with many de Bono books, he reworks many of his old techniques, so you may have seen some of them before.**

What the Dog Saw Malcolm Gladwell

WHAT THE BOOK SAYS

- This is not a book on one theme – it is a compendium of his best essays for the *New Yorker* magazine over the last 10 years or so, organised into three sections: i) Obsessives, pioneers, and other varieties of minor genius; ii) Theories, predictions and diagnoses; iii) Personality, character and intelligence.
- The title refers to his take on how Cesar Millan, aka the Dog Whisperer, does what he does. Gladwell is more interested in the dog's perspective, and it transpires that the dog's response is mainly down to Millan's body language.
- He teases out scores of curiosities, including:
  - □ Most things are not interesting
  - □ Perfection is plural: everybody has a different version of it
  - □ Heinz Ketchup remains unchanged and unbeatable because it covers every one of the five tastes we crave – salt, sweet, sour, bitter and umami – all in one product (umami is a proteiny, full-bodied taste)
  - □ The Clairol strapline *'Does she or doesn't she?'*, followed by L'Oreal's *'Because I'm worth it'* plots the course of female liberation in the twentieth century
  - □ Progress often comes in advance of understanding, as with the invention of the contraceptive pill
  - □ A puzzle is not the same as a mystery. Osama bin Laden's whereabouts (at the time of writing) were a puzzle. How Enron collapsed is actually a mystery

WHAT'S GOOD ABOUT IT

- The wisdom keeps coming:
  - □ Stop managing problems and start ending them
  - □ Solving issues means connecting the dots and spotting the sequence. Many people just can't do it. They just see ink blots like the Rorschach Test (he was the twentieth-century Swiss psychiatrist who invented it)

- □ Claiming retrospectively that something was coherent or made sense all along is a case of creeping determinism (x apparently determined y, but it didn't really). This affects many business case histories, and much journalism
- □ Choking is loss of instinct (a tennis player reverts to thinking about each shot and loses the game). Panic is reversion to instinct (a diver grabs instinctively for a companion's air supply without realising they can share and both be fine)
- □ Risk homeostasis is where changes intended to make a system safer actually make it worse. When ABS brakes are fitted to cars people drive faster and have more accidents, because they think they are safer
- □ There is no such thing as inherent genius. There are as many late bloomers as there are child prodigies
- □ If everyone has to think outside the box, maybe the box needs fixing

WHAT YOU HAVE TO WATCH
- All the essays are available for free on his website, so you don't have to pay £20.

Why Business People Speak Like Idiots FUGERE, HARDAWAY & WARSHAWSKY

WHAT THE BOOK SAYS
- Bull has become the official language of business. Every day we are bombarded by an endless stream of filtered, antiseptic, jargon-filled corporate speak, all of which makes it harder to get heard, be authentic, and have fun.
- It doesn't have to be that way. This is a guide for those who want to get on without leaving their personality at the door.
- The second people get to work, they usually trade the wit and warmth of their normal voices for a corporate stamp of approval and the comfort of conformity.

- This is not because of some evil corporate conspiracy. It's the result of four traps:
  1. *Obscurity trap:* jargon, wordiness, and evasiveness
     This can be overcome by avoiding long and pointless words, keeping everything short, and coming to the point.
  2. *Anonymity trap:* corporate clones sound like everyone else
     This can be overcome by ditching templates, keeping imperfection in presentations to show humanity, using humour, and picking up the phone.
  3. *Hard-sell trap:* fear, habit and bad role models are all to blame
     This can be overcome by using the 'non-sell sell', by kicking the habit of the relentlessly happy messenger, and by apologising properly for mistakes.
  4. *Tedium trap:* most people ignore things: *'And this is interesting because?'*
     You can overcome this by entertaining people, bringing things to life, using their point to make yours, telling stories, and having style.
- If you can rise above these traps, it is possible to capture people's imagination, stir their enthusiasm, and tell them the truth. Even at work.

WHAT'S GOOD ABOUT IT
- You can rattle through this book fast, laugh at the absurdity of much work language, and pick up some helpful tips for railing against the conformity of work.

WHAT YOU HAVE TO WATCH
- It is extremely American, with all the examples to match.
- It is very much a rant, so it's like listening to someone having an outburst in a pub, with a few good ideas thrown in.

Why We Buy PACO UNDERHILL

WHAT THE BOOK SAYS

- There is a science of shopping. It can be understood by intense scrutiny of how people behave in the retail environment.
- The mechanics of shopping shows, among other things, that there is a twilight zone in the entrance of stores that people go straight past; that having two hands restricts their options; that they have real trouble reading signs; that they move in certain clearly defined ways; and that they shift around all the time.
- Understanding these dynamics and making small changes can lead to massive increases in sales and profits.
- People want to see, feel and touch most items they might buy, and yet many store designs, and a lot of packaging, prevents them from doing so. These sensory elements are often ignored in the shopping process.
- Shopping is defined as experiencing that portion of the world that has been deemed for sale – it is an activity in its own right, not just the acquisition of necessities.
- The confusion index measures how baffled shoppers are, and the interception rate measures how often they interact with staff.
- The butt-brush factor determines how closely packed merchandise is – women in particular hate it when people squeeze past them.

WHAT'S GOOD ABOUT IT

- Shoppers love touch, mirrors, discovery, talking, recognition and bargains.
- Shoppers dislike too many mirrors, having to ask dumb questions, dipping down to pick things up, goods out of stock, obscure price tags and intimidating service.
- Examples of small tweaks and details in the retail environment include:
  - ☐ The CEO who thought his conversion rate was perfect, only to find it was 48 per cent

□ Store owners who think people spend 10 minutes in-store, when in fact it is two

□ Giving people a basket when their hands are full means they will buy more

□ Sixty-five per cent of men who try something on buy it, but only 25 per cent of women

□ The dressing room is the most important room in a store, but has the least investment

□ Waiting time can be 'bent' by human interaction, orderliness of queuing, companionship and diversion – these make people wait longer more happily

WHAT YOU HAVE TO WATCH

- It is perhaps not surprisingly hugely in favour of shopping, and not everyone will agree with this.
- The author is not a fan of online shopping, and says so at some length.

Zag MARTY NEUMEIER

WHAT THE BOOK SAYS

- In an age of me-too products and instant communications, keeping up with the competition is no longer a winning strategy. You have to out-position, out-manoeuvre, and out-design everyone else.
- When everybody zigs, zag. Radical differentiation is the number one strategy of high-performance brands.
- There is a 17-step process for working all this out:
  1. Who are you?
  2. What do you do?
  3. What's your vision?
  4. What wave are you riding?
  5. Who shares the brandscape?
  6. What makes you the 'only'?
  7. What should you add or subtract?
  8. Who loves you?
  9. Who's the enemy?
  10. What do they call you?

11. How do you explain yourself?
12. How do you spread the word?
13. How do people engage with you?
14. What do they experience?
15. How do you earn their loyalty?
16. How do you extend your success?
17. How do you protect your portfolio?

WHAT'S GOOD ABOUT IT

- This is a short, inspirational book. You can follow the sequence and apply it to a brand immediately. Each step has a number of subsidiary questions.
- It tells you how to 'find your zag', then design it, and renew it.
- The main set up is that everything is speeding up, the real competition is clutter so don't offer more, offer different. Look for white space and 'hit 'em where they ain't'.
- Companies today have no choice but to connect to the three insatiable demands of business: free, perfect and now.
- The Intrusiveness Death Spiral is a provocative concept whereby traditional advertising achieves short-term gains at the expense of long-term effectiveness:
  1. Industry creates more intrusive ads
  2. Audience buys in short term
  3. Audience tunes out in long term
  4. Advertising becomes less effective

WHAT YOU HAVE TO WATCH

- It is inventively packaged, but we have seen most of these questions before.

Online resources

Hot, Flat, and Crowded, Thomas Friedman:
www.thomaslfriedman.com

Chaotics, Kotler & Caslione:
www.kotlermarketing.com

The Little Big Things, Tom Peters:
www.tompeters.com

The Spirit Level Delusion, Christopher Snowdon:
www.spiritleveldelusion.com

Drive, Daniel Pink:
www.danpink.com

The Undercover Economist, Tim Harford:
www.timharford.com

Discover Your Inner Economist, Tyler Cowen:
www.marginalrevolution.com

Predictably Irrational, Dan Ariely:
www.danariely.com

Why We Buy, Paco Underhill:
www.pacounderhill.com

Buyology, Martin Lindstrom:
www.martinlindstrom.com

The Great Stagnation, Tyler Cowen:
www.marginalrevolution.com

The Living Company, Arie de Geus:
www.ariedegeus.com

Rework, Fried & Hansson:
www.37signals.com

Everything is Miscellaneous, David Weinberger:
www.everythingismiscellaneous.com

Bad Science, Ben Goldacre:
www.badscience.net

Predicting Market Success, Robert Passikoff:
www.brandkeys.com

Creative Disruption, Simon Waldman:
www.simonwaldman.net

Microtrends, Mark J. Penn:
www.microtrending.com

Socialnomics, Erik Qualman:
www.socialnomics.net

Cognitive Surplus, Clay Shirky:
www.shirky.com

Poke the Box, Seth Godin:
www.sethgodin.com

Obliquity, John Kay:
www.johnkay.com

The Business Playground, Stewart & Simmons:
www.businessplayground.com

Think!, Edward de Bono:
www.edwarddebono.com

Sticky Wisdom, Matt Kingdon et al.:
www.whatifinnovation.com

Zag, Marty Neumeier:
www.liquidagency.com

Exceptional Service, Exceptional Profit, Inghilleri & Solomon:
www.leonardoinghilleri.com

Why Business People Speak Like Idiots, Brian Fugure et al.:
www.fightthebull.com

What the Dog Saw, Malcolm Gladwell:
www.gladwell.com

BIBLIOGRAPHY

CHAPTER 1

Friedman, Thomas L. *Hot, Flat, and Crowded*. London: Penguin, 2009.

Kotler, Philip, and John A. Caslione. *Chaotics*. New York: Amacom, 2009.

Peters, Tom. *The Little Big Things*. New York: John Wiley, 2010.

Snowdon, Christopher. *The Spirit Level Delusion*. London: Little Dice, 2010.

Hill, Dan. *Emotionomics*. London: Kogan Page, 2008.

Pink, Daniel H. *Drive*. Edinburgh: Canongate, 2010.

CHAPTER 2

Harford, Tim. *The Undercover Economist*. London: Little Brown, 2009.

Cowen, Tyler. *Discover Your Inner Economist*. New York: Plume, 2007.

Ariely, Dan. *Predictably Irrational*. London: Harper Collins, 2009.

Schwartz, Barry. *The Paradox of Choice*. New York: Harper Perennial, 2004.

Underhill, Paco. *Why We Buy*. New York: Simon & Schuster, 2009.

Lindstrom, Martin. *Buyology*. London: Random House, 2009.

Cowen, Tyler. *The Great Stagnation*. New York: Penguin, 2011.

CHAPTER 3

de Geus, Arie. *The Living Company*. London: Nicholas Brealey, 1998.

Fried, Jason, and David Heinemeier Hansson. *Rework*. London: Vermillion, 2010.

Miller, Peter. *Smart Swarm*. London: Collins, 2010.

Goffee, Robert, and Gareth Jones. *Clever*. Boston: Harvard Business Press, 2009.

Osterwalder, Alexander, and Yves Pigneur. *Business Model Generation*. New Jersey: John Wiley, 2010.

Pressfield, Steven. *Do The Work*. The Domino Project, 2011.

Templar, Richard. *The Rules of Management*. Harlow: Pearson, 2005.

CHAPTER 4

Lucas, Bill. *Revolution*. Carmarthen: Crown House, 2009.

Weinberger, David. *Everything is Miscellaneous*. New York: Holt, 2007.

Goldacre, Ben. *Bad Science*. London: Harper Perennial, 2009.

Passikoff, Robert. *Predicting Market Success*. New Jersey: John Wiley, 2006.

Waldman, Simon. *Creative Disruption*. Harlow: Pearson, 2010.

Penn, Mark J. *Microtrends*. London: Penguin, 2008.

Qualman, Erik. *Socialnomics*. New Jersey: John Wiley, 2009.

CHAPTER 5

Shirky, Clay. *Cognitive Surplus*. London: Allen Lane, 2010.

Godin, Seth. *Poke the Box*. The Domino Project, 2011.

Kay, John. *Obliquity*. London: Profile, 2010.

Stewart, Dave, and Mark Simmons. *The Business Playground*. Harlow: Pearson, 2010.

de Bono, Edward, *Think!* London: Vermillion, 2009.

Kingdon, Matt, et al. *Sticky Wisdom*. Chichester: Capstone, 2002.

Neumeier, Marty. *Zag*. Berkeley: New Riders, 2007.

CHAPTER 6

Hitchings, Henry. *The Language Wars*. London: John Murray, 2011.

Frankfurt, Harry G. *On Bullshit*. New Jersey: Princeton University Press, 2005.

Inghilleri, Leonardo, and Micah Solomon. *Exceptional Service, Exceptional Profit*. New York: Amacom, 2010.

Fugere, Brian, et al. *Why Business People Speak Like Idiots*. New York: Free Press, 2005.

Edmonds, Graham. *Bad Language*. London: Southbank, 2008.

Gladwell, Malcolm. *What the Dog Saw*. London: Allen Lane, 2009.

Index